INTEGRITY'S

iWORSHIP/CONNECT
LIVE YOUR WORSHIP

2	Amazed
7	Blessed Be Your Name
14	Came To My Rescue
20	Come, Now Is The Time To Worship
26	Days Of Elijah
32	Everlasting God
38	Friend Of God
45	From The Inside Out
52	God You Reign
58	Healer
64	Here I Am To Worship
74	Holy Is The Lord
80	Hosanna
86	Hosanna (Praise Is Rising)
94	How Great Is Our God
67	How He Loves
98	Hungry (Falling On My Knees)
104	I Am Free
112	In Christ Alone/The Solid Rock
119	Lead Me To The Cross
124	Love The Lord
132	Mighty To Save
148	Moving Forward
156	Open The Eyes Of My Heart
164	Revelation Song
170	Today Is The Day
178	Trading My Sorrows
186	You Are Good
194	Your Grace Is Enough
141	Your Name

ISBN 973-1-4234-8315-1

HAL•LEONARD®
CORPORATION
7777 W. BLUEMOUND RD. P.O. BOX 13819 MILWAUKEE, WI 53213

Visit Hal Leonard Online at
www.halleonard.com

AMAZED

Words and Music by
JARED ANDERSON

Moderately slow

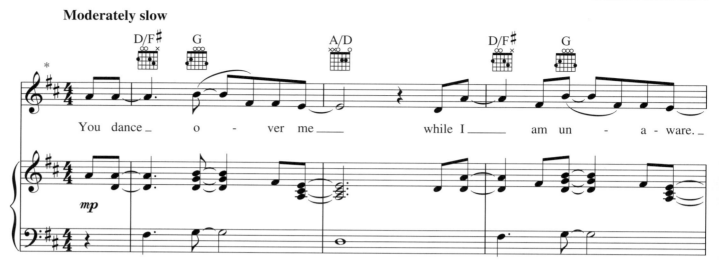

You dance _ o - ver me _ while I _ am un - a - ware. _

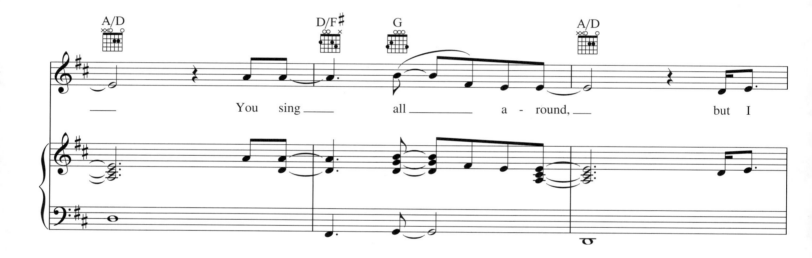

_ You sing _ all _ a - round, _ but I

nev - er hear _ the sound. _ Lord, I'm a - mazed _____ by You. _

Recorded a half step lower.

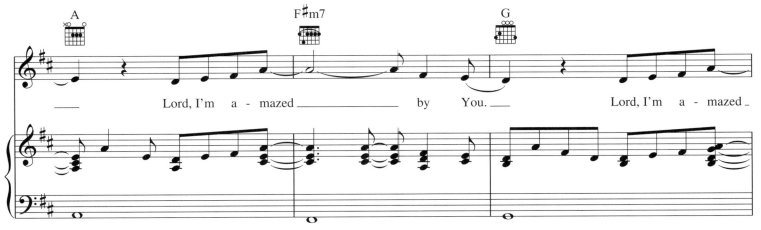

Lord, I'm a - mazed _____ by You. ____ Lord, I'm a - mazed ____

_____ by You, ____ how You love ____ me.

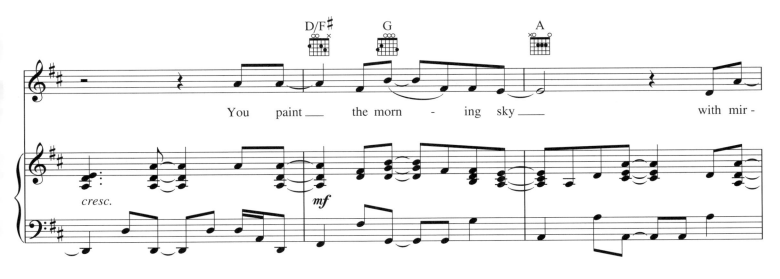

You paint ____ the morn - ing sky ____ with mir -

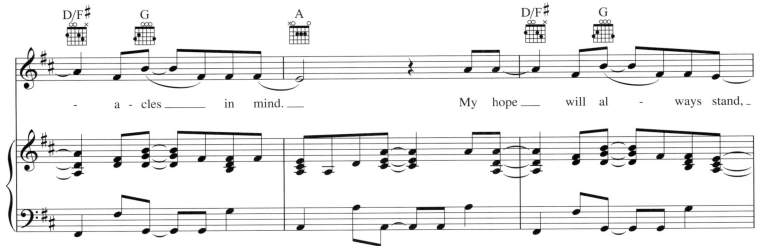

- a - cles _____ in mind. ____ My hope ____ will al - ways stand, ____

You hold ___ me in ___ Your hand. ___ Lord, I'm a - mazed ___

___ by You. ___ Lord, I'm a - mazed ___ by You. ___

___ Lord, I'm a - mazed ___ by You, ___ how You love ___

___ me. How wide, ___

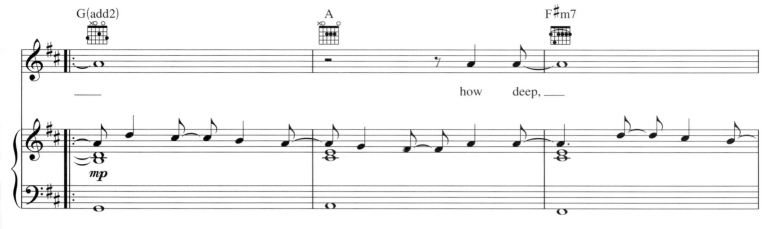

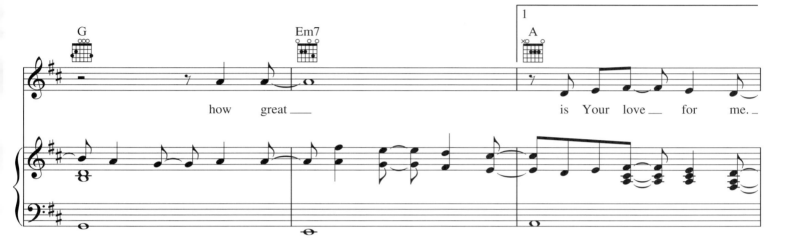

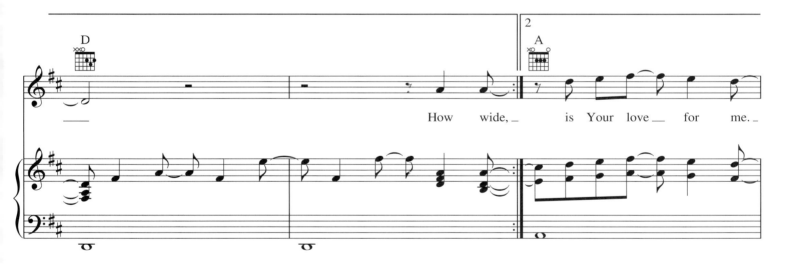

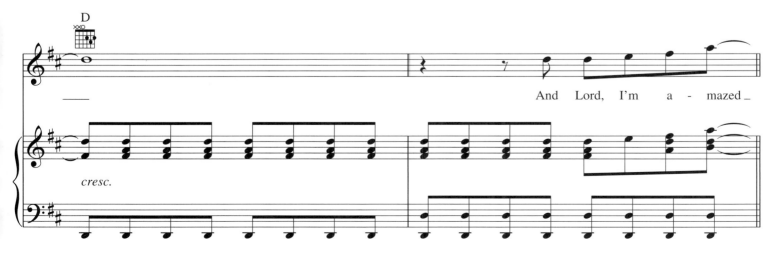

BLESSED BE YOUR NAME

Words and Music by MATT REDMAN
and BETH REDMAN

* Recorded a half step lower.

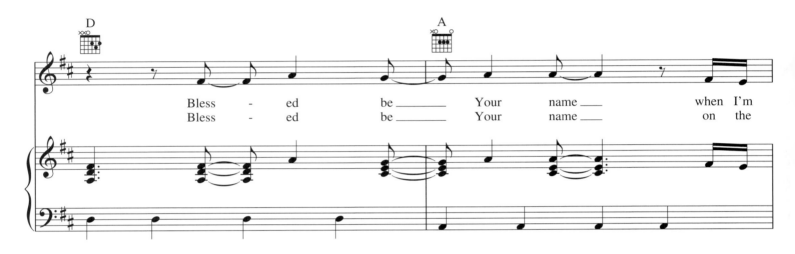

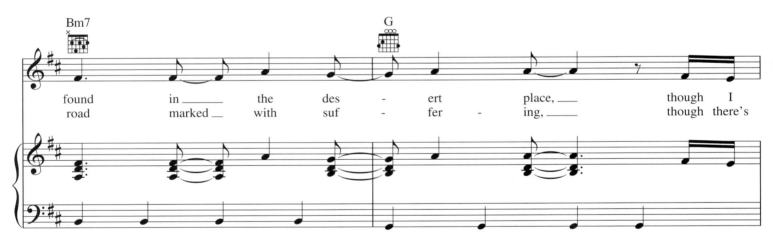

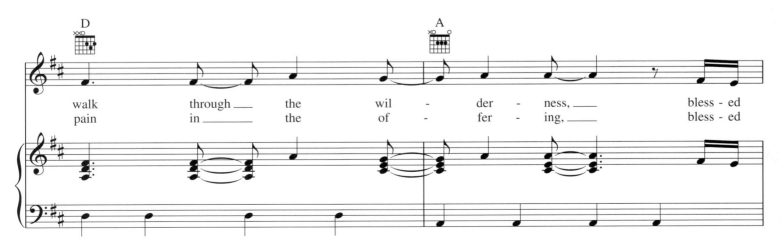

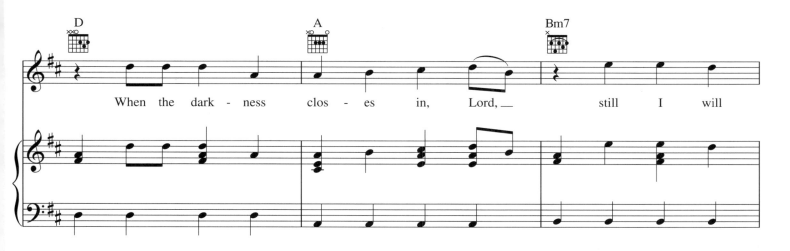

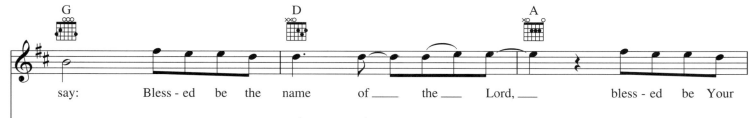

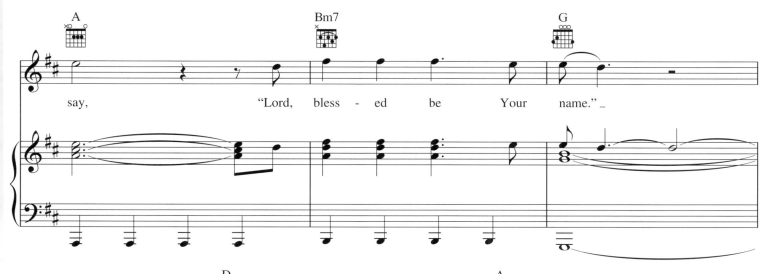

say, "Lord, bless - ed be Your name." _

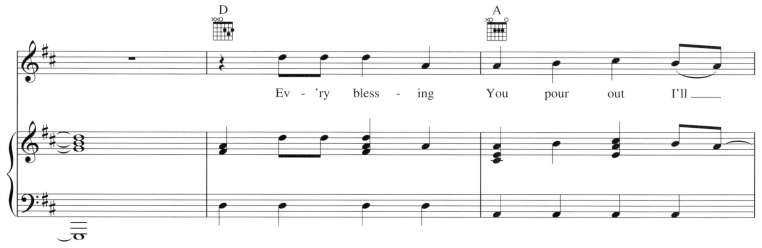

Ev - 'ry bless - ing You pour out I'll _____

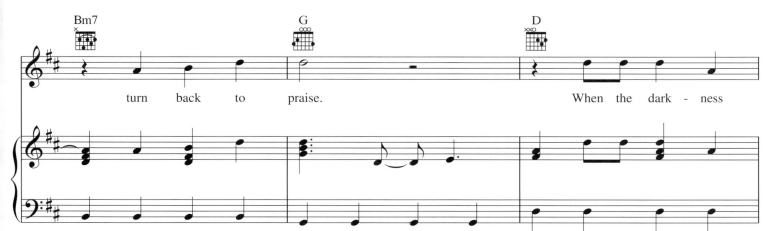

turn back to praise. When the dark - ness

clos - es in, Lord, _ still I'm gon - na say: _ Bless - ed be the

name of ____ the ____ Lord, ____ bless - ed be Your name, Je -

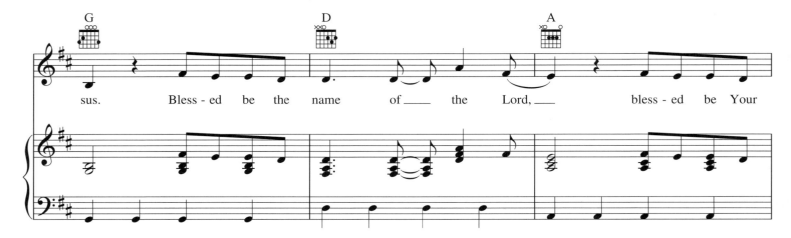

sus. Bless - ed be the name of ____ the Lord, ____ bless - ed be Your

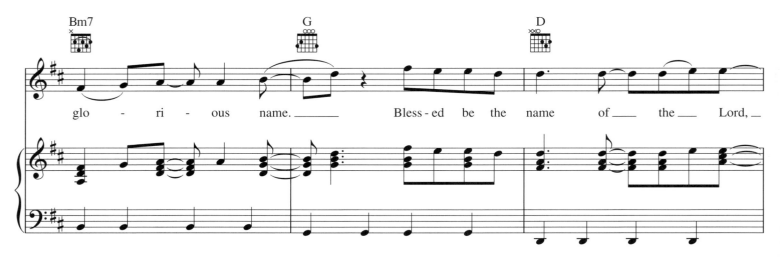

glo - ri - ous name. _____ Bless - ed be the name of ____ the ____ Lord, _

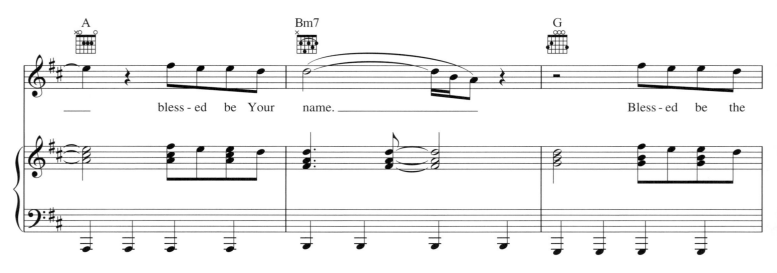

____ bless - ed be Your name. _____ Bless - ed be the

CAME TO MY RESCUE

Words and Music by MARTY SAMPSON,
DYLAN THOMAS and JOEL DAVIES

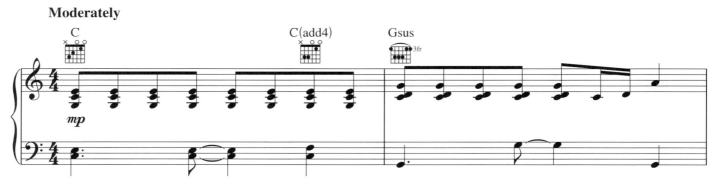

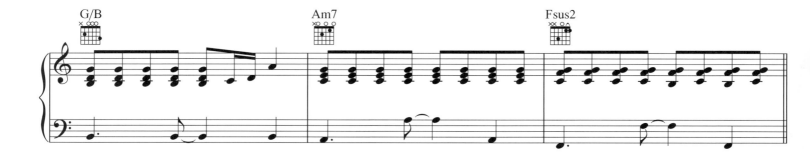

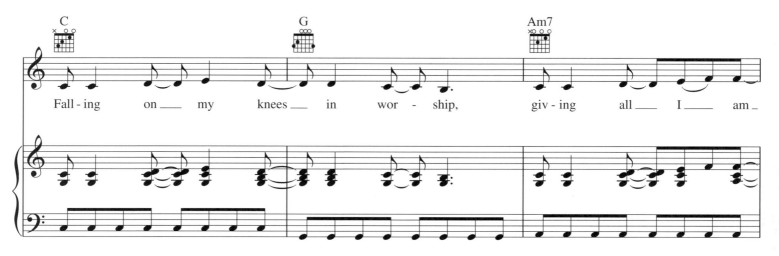

Fall-ing on ___ my knees ___ in wor-ship, giv-ing all I ___ am ___

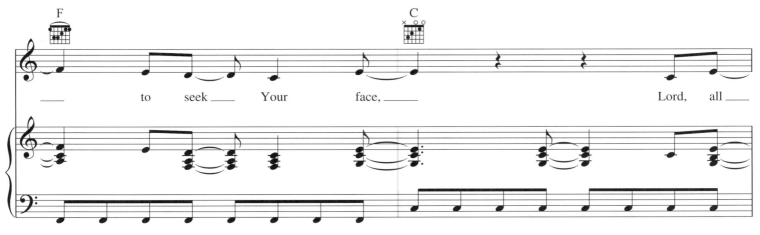

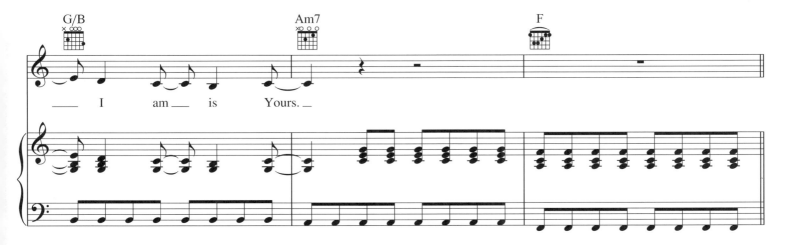

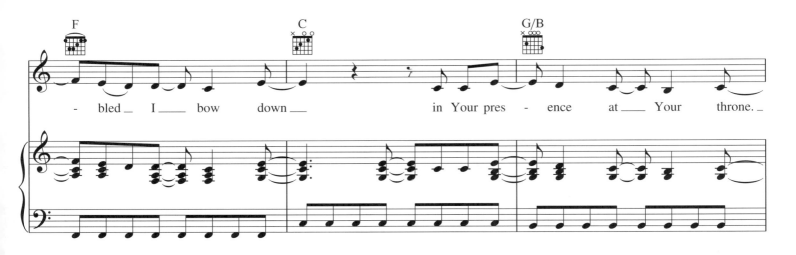

I ___ called, You an-swered, _____

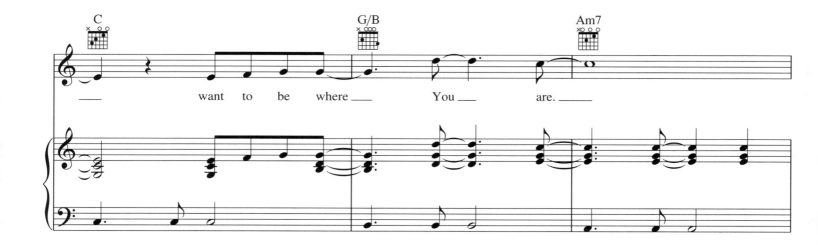

and You came to my res-cue, and I ___

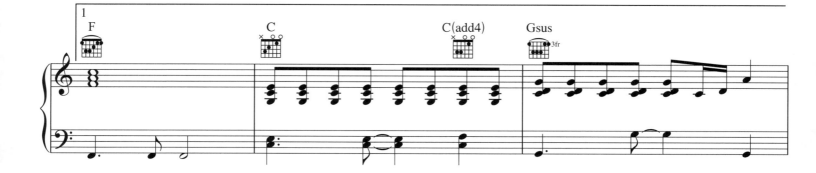

want to be where ___ You ___ are. _____

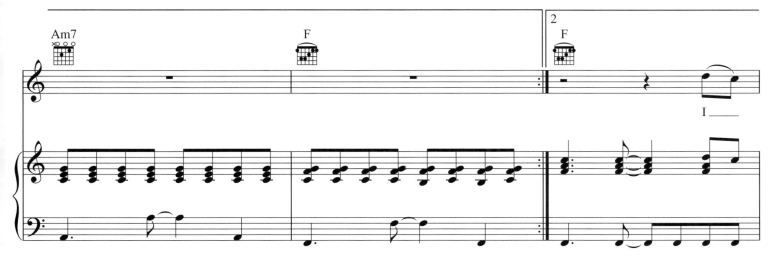

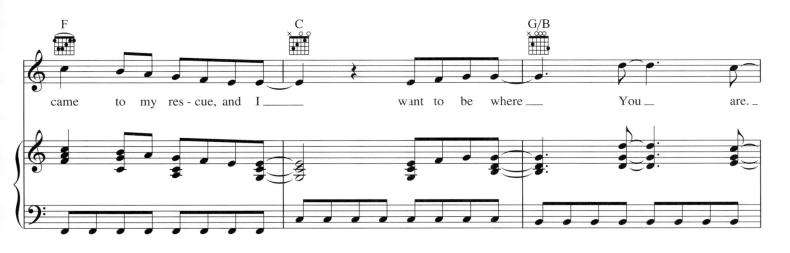

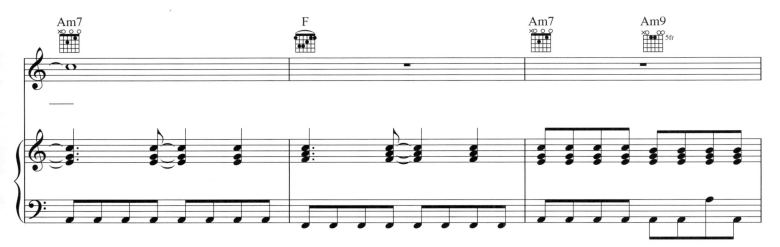

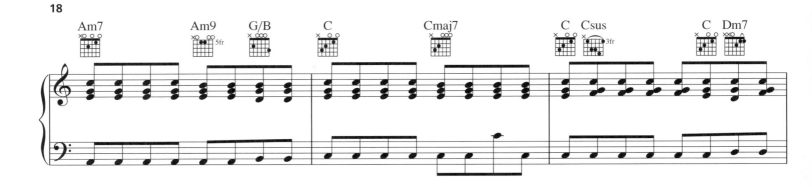

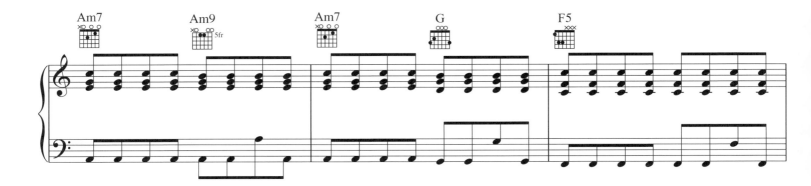

In my life, be lift-ed ___ high. ___

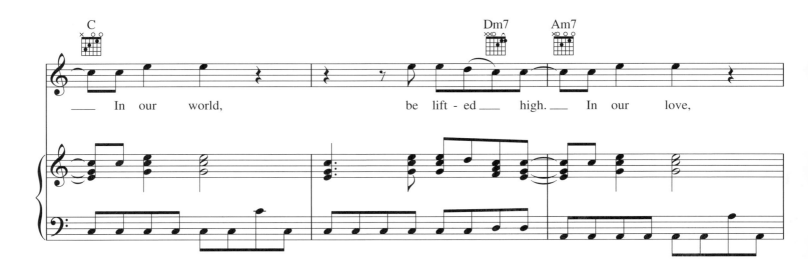

___ In our world, be lift-ed ___ high. ___ In our love,

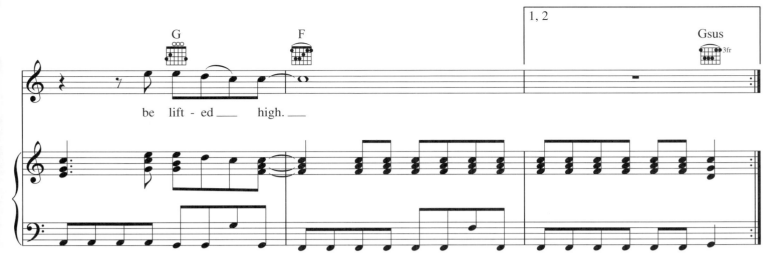

be lift - ed ____ high. ____

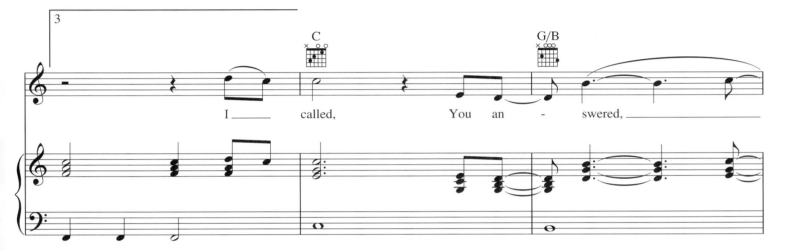

I ____ called, You an - swered, _____

____ and You came to my res - cue, and I ____ want to be where ____

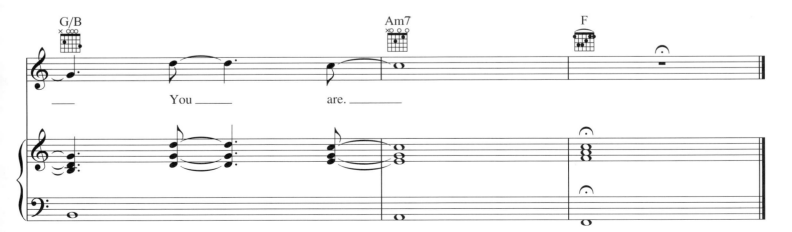

____ You ____ are. ____

COME, NOW IS THE TIME TO WORSHIP

Words and Music by
BRIAN DOERKSEN

Driving Rock

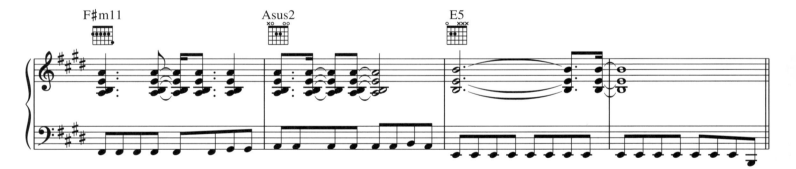

Come, now is the time __ to wor -

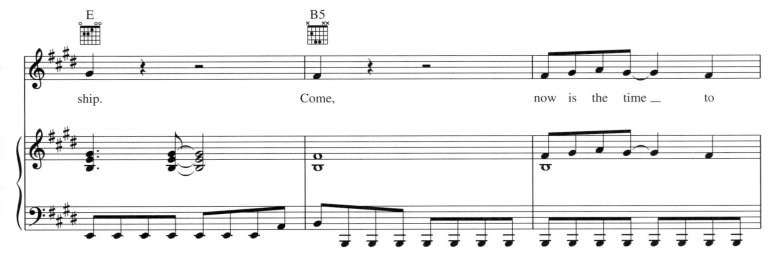

ship.   Come,   now is the time ___ to

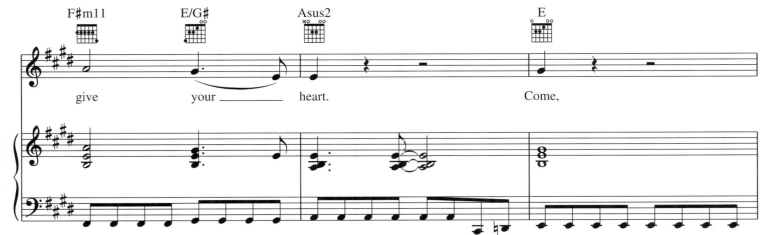

give   your _____ heart.   Come,

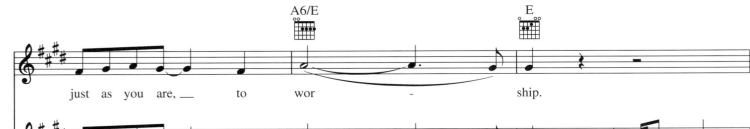

just as you are, ___ to wor - ship.

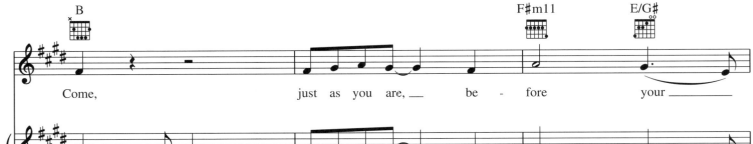

Come,   just as you are, ___ be - fore   your _____

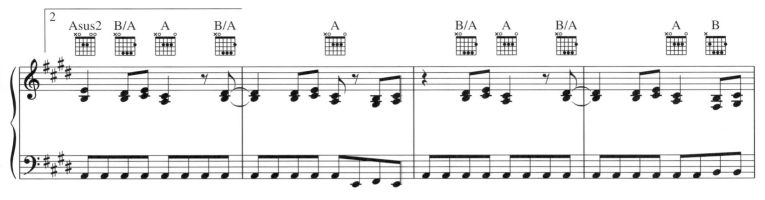

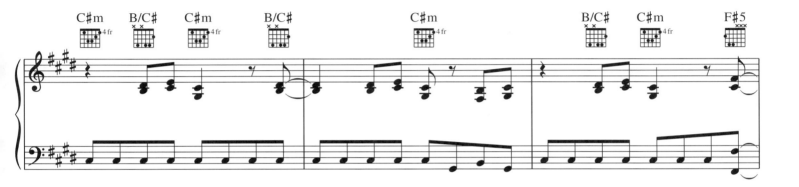

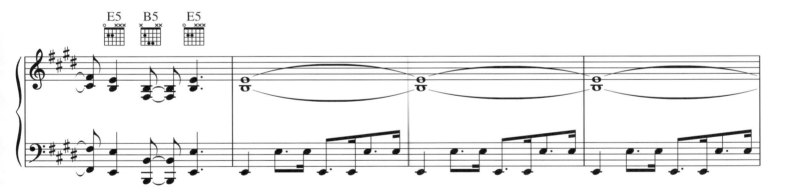

Ooh, _____

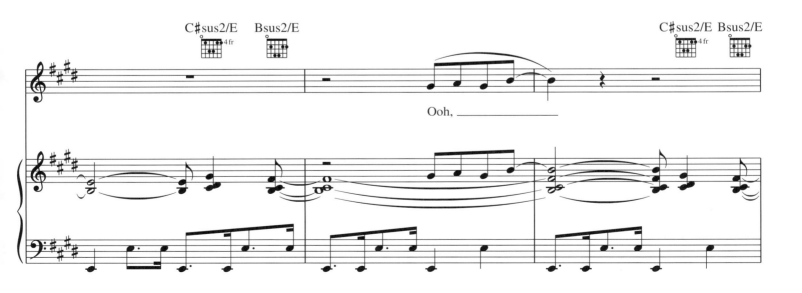

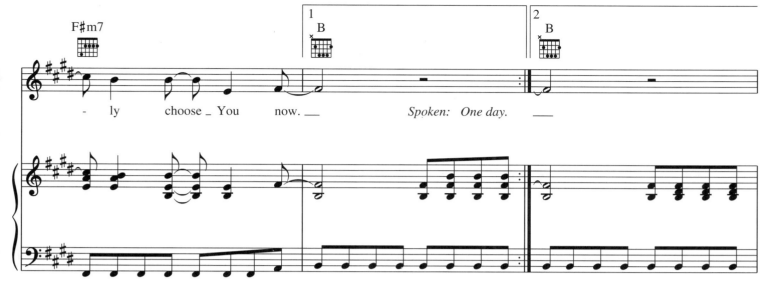

- ly choose _ You now. _ *Spoken: One day.* _

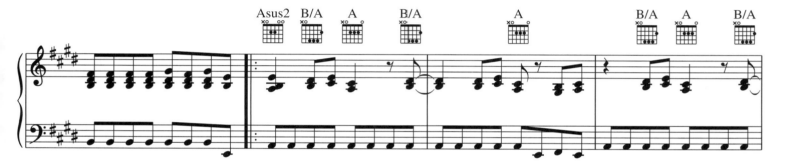

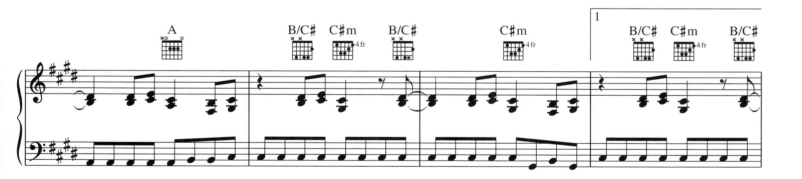

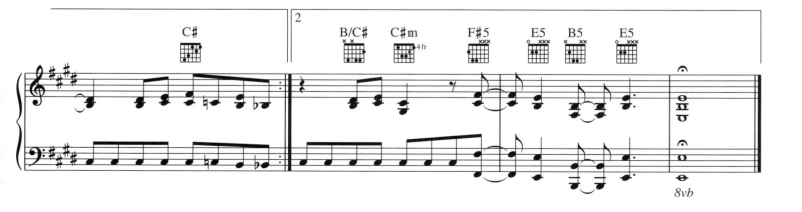

8vb

DAYS OF ELIJAH

Words and Music by
ROBIN MARK

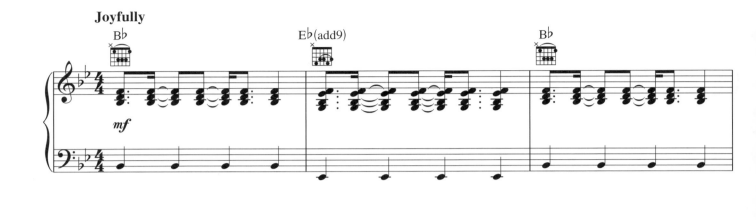

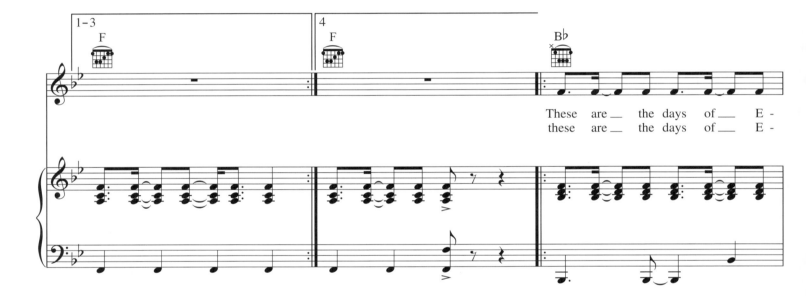

These are __ the days of __ E-
these are __ the days of __ E-

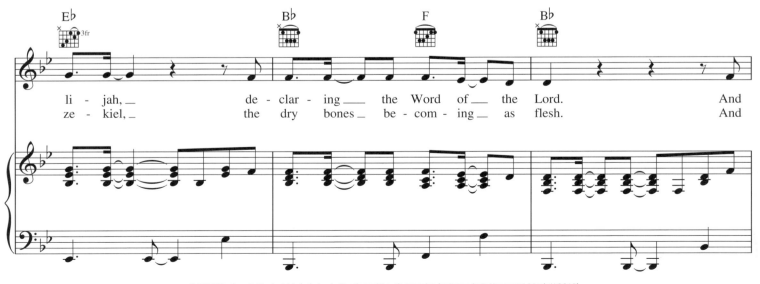

li - jah, __ de - clar - ing __ the Word of __ the Lord. And
ze - kiel, __ the dry bones __ be - com - ing __ as flesh. And

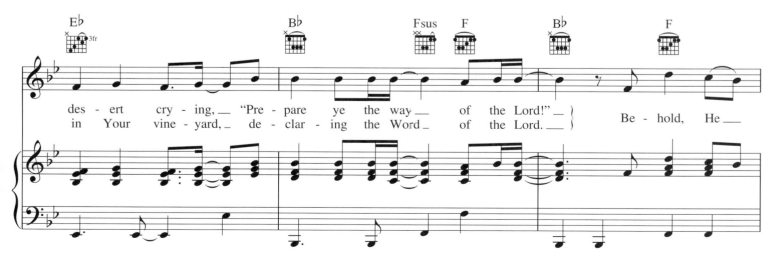

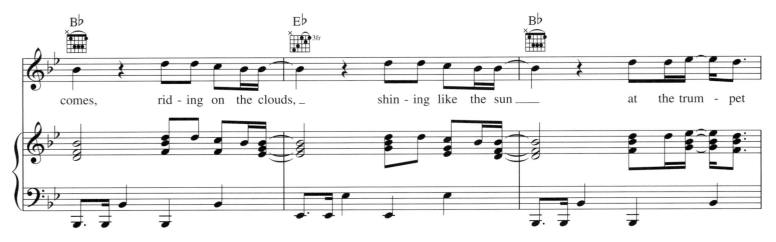

comes, rid-ing on the clouds, __ shin-ing like the sun ____ at the trum-pet

call. Lift your __ voice, it's the year of Ju-bi-lee, ____ and out of Zi-on's

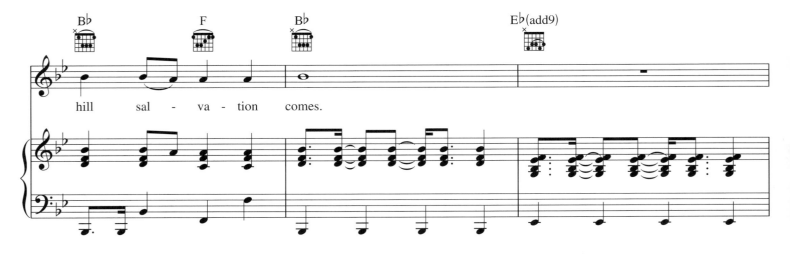

hill sal - va - tion comes.

And

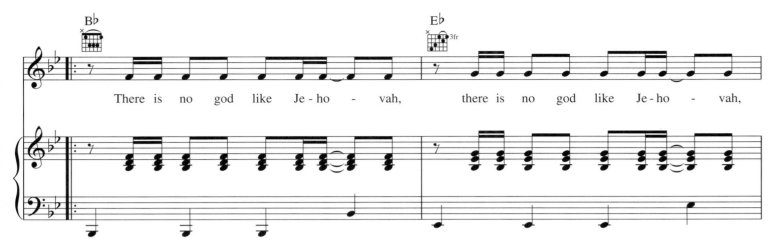

There is no god like Je-ho-vah, there is no god like Je-ho-vah,

there is no god like Je-ho-vah, there is no god like Je-ho-vah!

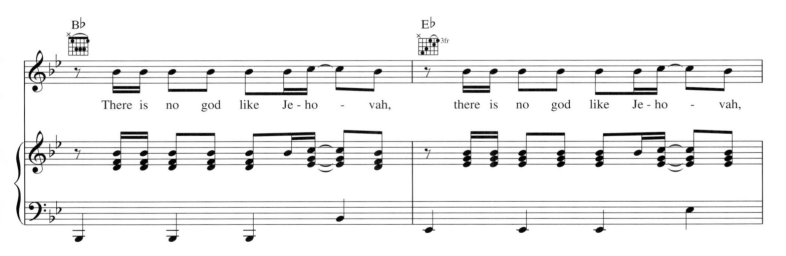

There is no god like Je-ho-vah, there is no god like Je-ho-vah,

there is no god like Je-ho-vah, there is no god like Je-ho-vah!

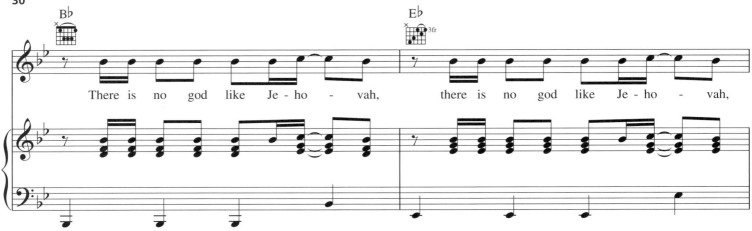

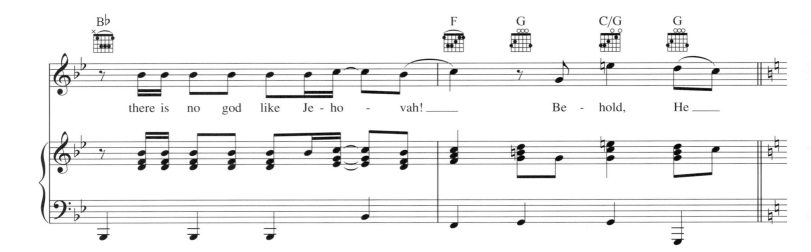

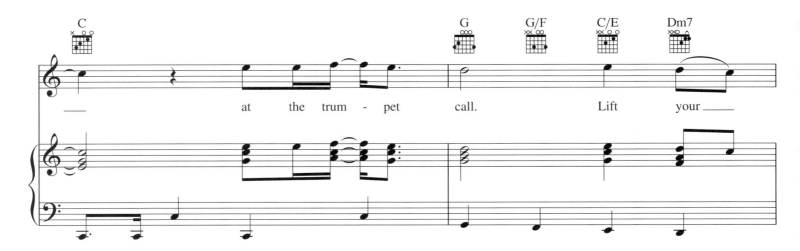

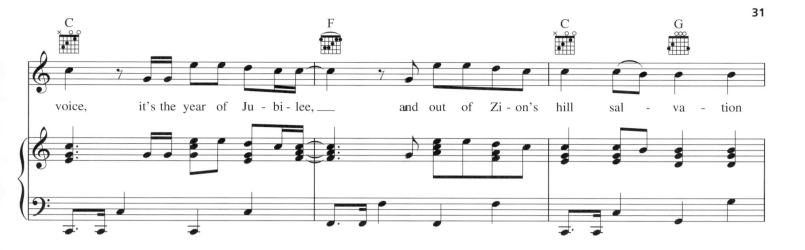

voice, it's the year of Ju - bi - lee, ___ and out of Zi - on's hill sal - va - tion

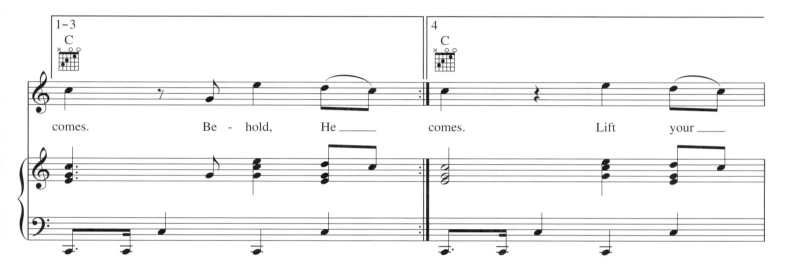

comes. Be - hold, He ___ comes. Lift your ___

voice, it's the year of Ju - bi - lee, ___ and out of Zi - on's hill sal - va - tion

comes.

EVERLASTING GOD

Words and Music by BRENTON BROWN
and KEN RILEY

Recorded a half step lower.

up - on the Lord. Our God, _____ You reign _____ for - ev -

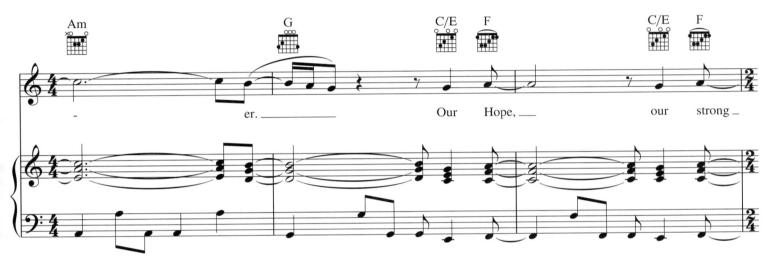

- er. _____ Our Hope, ___ our strong _

_ De - liv - er - er. _____

You are ___ the ev - er - last - ing God, ___ the ev -

-er - last - ing God. ___ You do ___ not faint, _ You ___

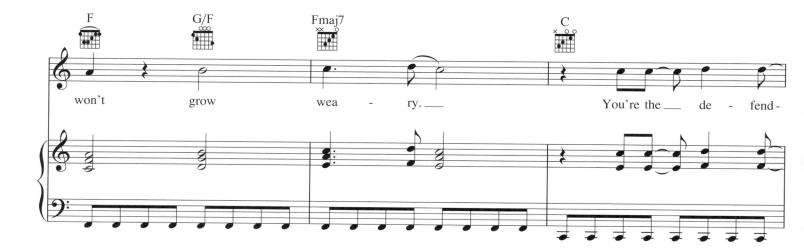

won't grow wea - ry. ___ You're the ___ de - fend-

-er of ___ the weak, ___ You com - fort those _ in need, _

___ You lift ___ us up ___ on ___ wings like

ea - gles. ___ ea - gles. ___

You are ___ the ev -

mp subito

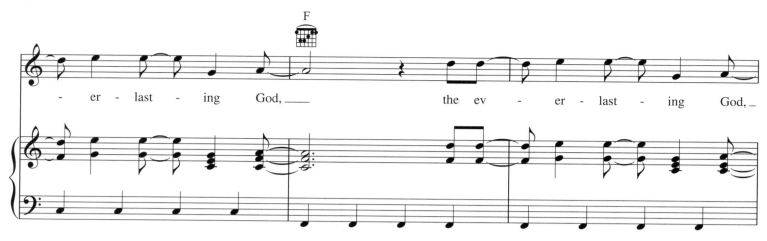

up - on the Lord,   wait ___ up - on the Lord,   wait ___ up - on the Lord. ___

You are ___ the ev - er - last - ing God, ___   the ev -

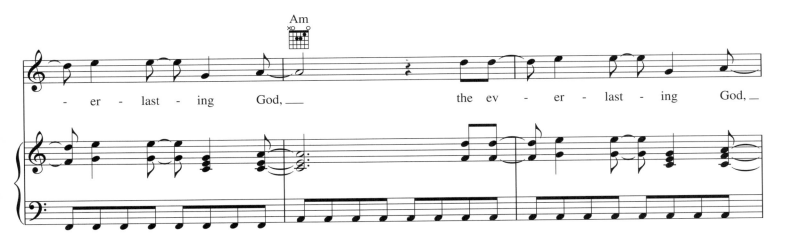

- er - last - ing God, ___   the ev - er - last - ing God, ___

___ the ev - er - last - ing.

FRIEND OF GOD

Words and Music by MICHAEL GUNGOR
and ISRAEL HOUGHTON

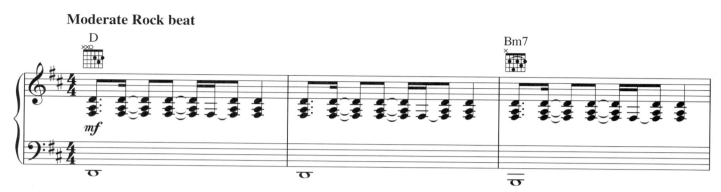

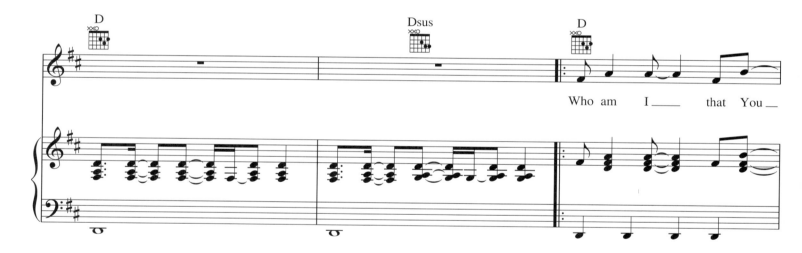

Who am I ___ that You ___

___ are mind-ful ___ of ___ me,

that You

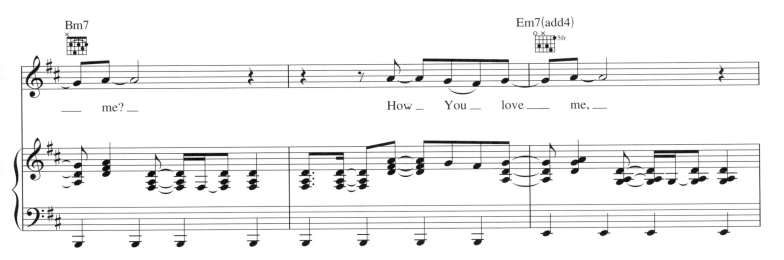

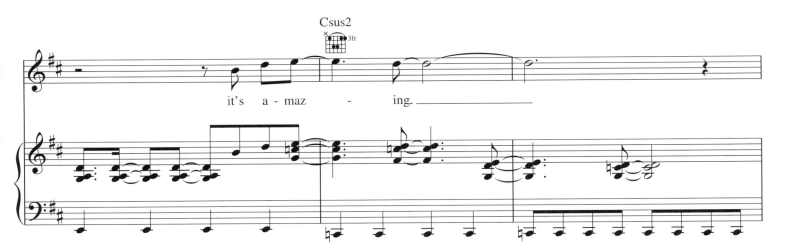

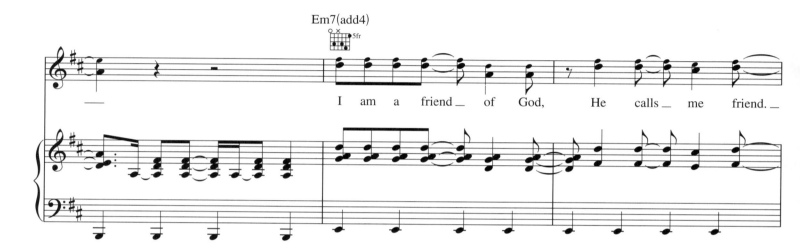

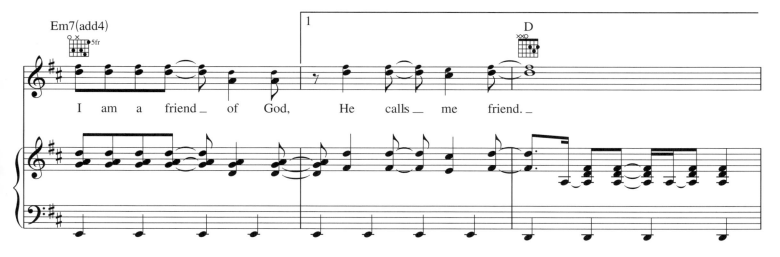

I am a friend __ of God, He calls __ me friend. __

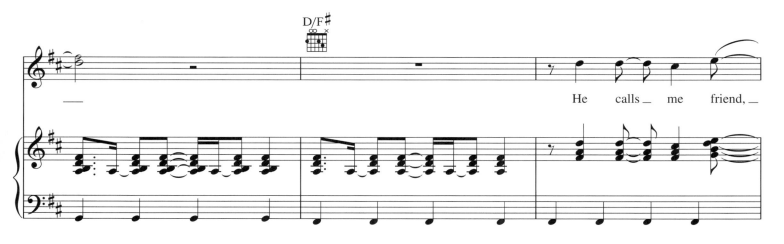

He calls __ me friend. _____

He calls __ me friend, __

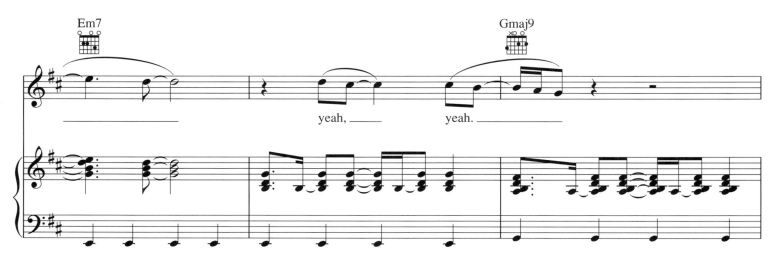

yeah, _____ yeah. _____

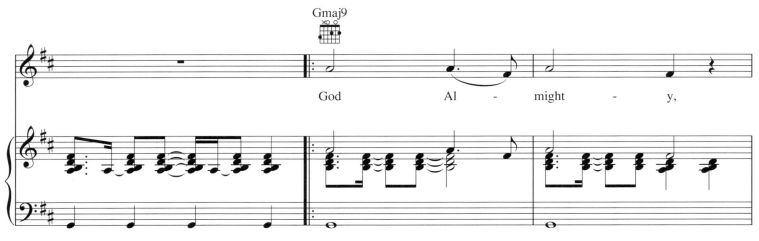

God Al - might - y,

Lord of _____ Glo - ry, You have

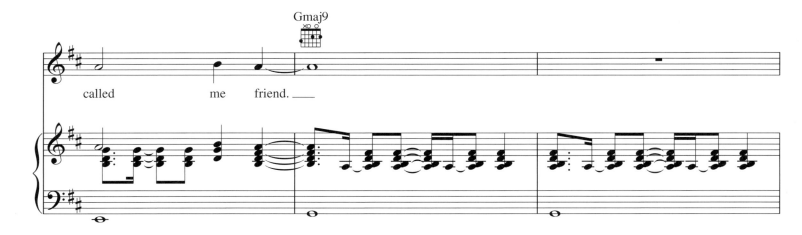

called me friend. ____

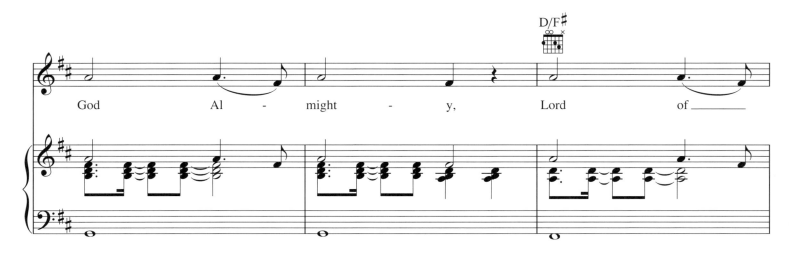

God Al - might - y, Lord of _____

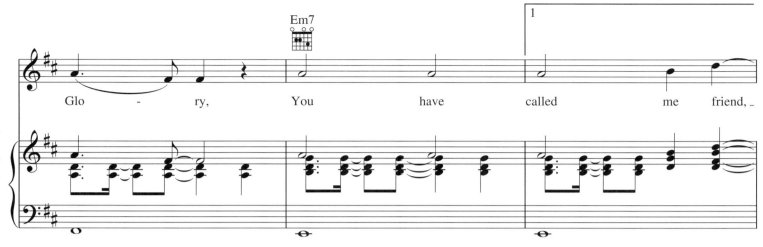

Glo - ry, You have called me friend, _

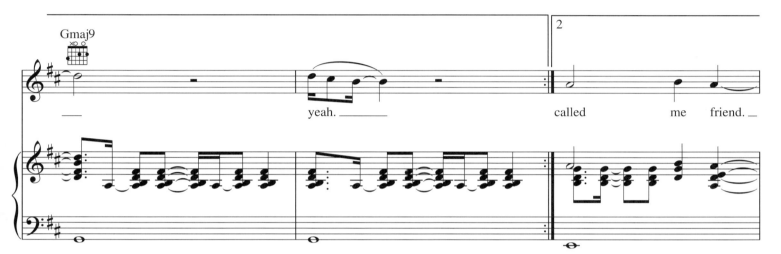

1
_ yeah. _____ 2 called me friend. _

_ I am a friend _ of God, _

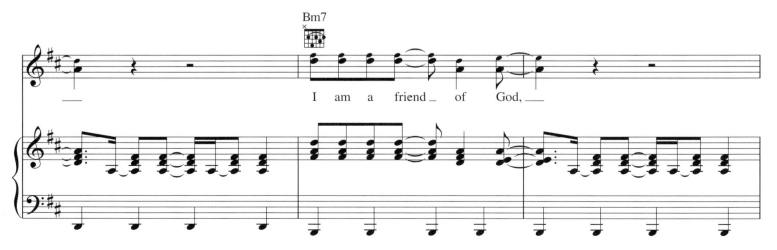

_ I am a friend _ of God, _

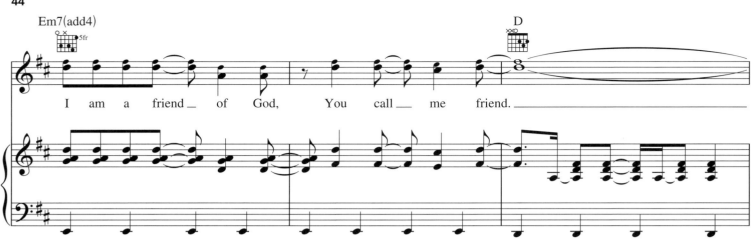

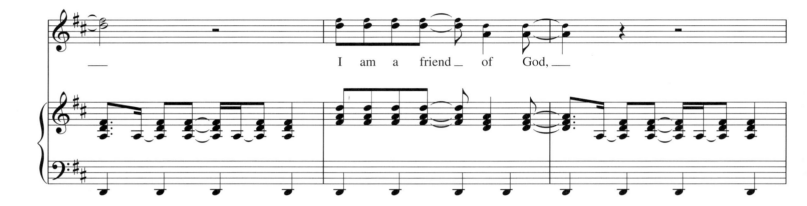

FROM THE INSIDE OUT

Words and Music by
JOEL HOUSTON

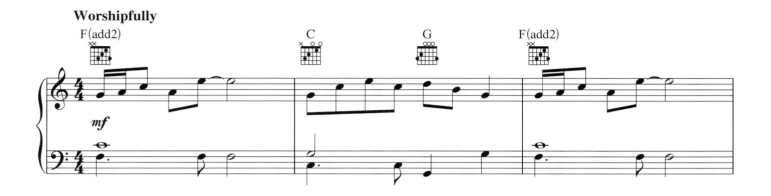

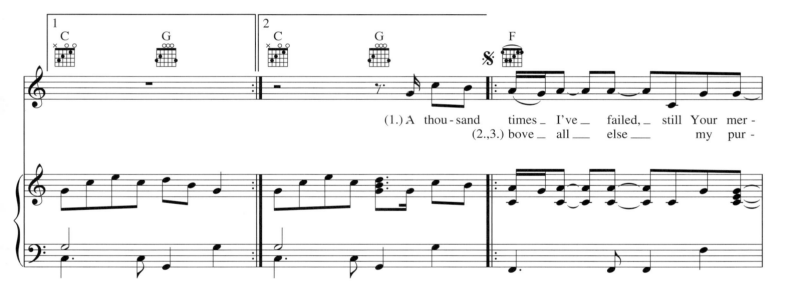

(1.) A thou-sand times _ I've _ failed, _ still Your mer-
(2.,3.) bove _ all _ else _ my pur-

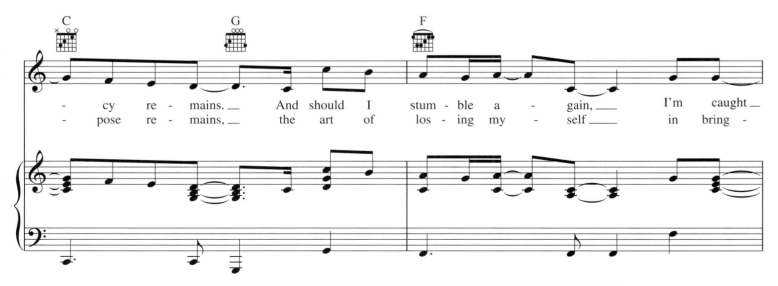

-cy re-mains. _ And should I stum-ble a-gain, _ I'm caught _
-pose re-mains, _ the art of los-ing my-self _ in bring -

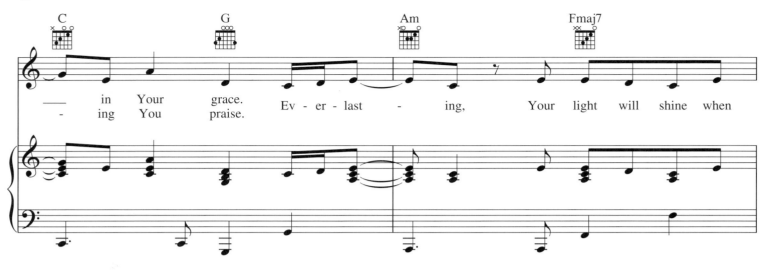

____ in Your grace. Ev-er-last - ing, Your light will shine when
-ing You praise.

all else fades. Nev-er-end - ing, Your glo-ry goes be-yond all fame.

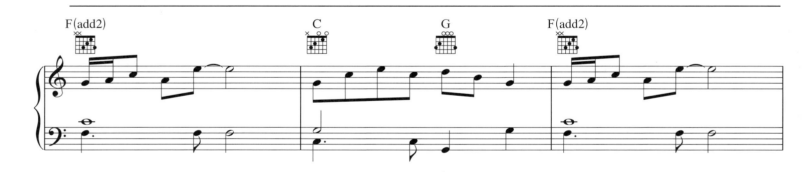

Your will a-yond all fame. In my heart and my soul, __

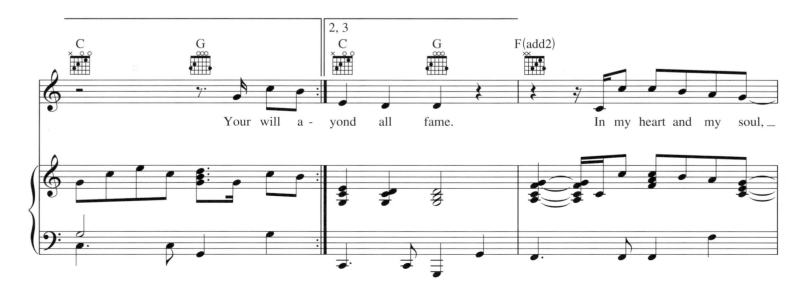

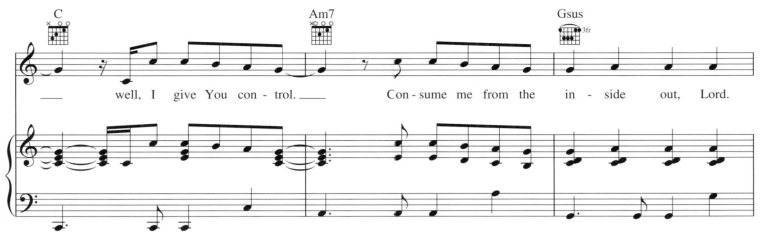

well, I give You con-trol. ___ Con-sume me from the in-side out, Lord.

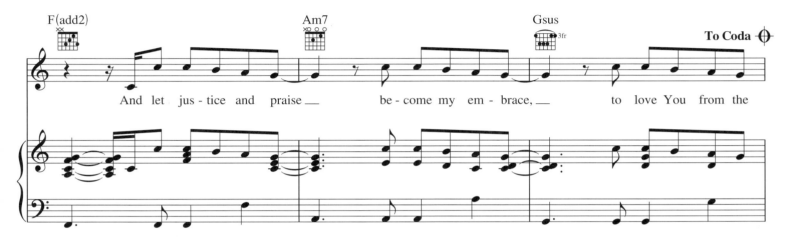

And let jus-tice and praise ___ be-come my em-brace, ___ to love You from the

To Coda ⊕

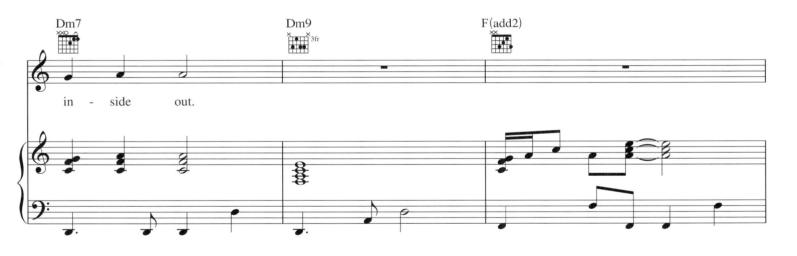

in - side out.

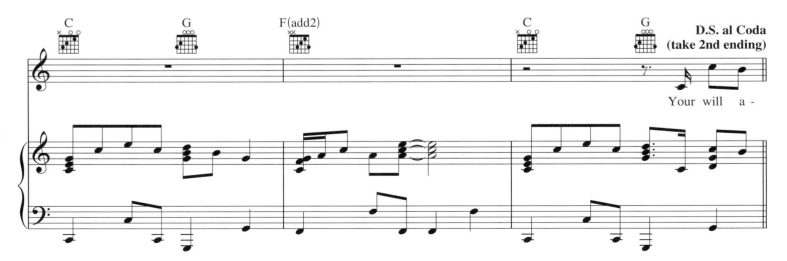

D.S. al Coda
(take 2nd ending)

Your will a-

in - side out. Ev - er - last - ing, Your light will shine when all else fades. Nev - er - end -

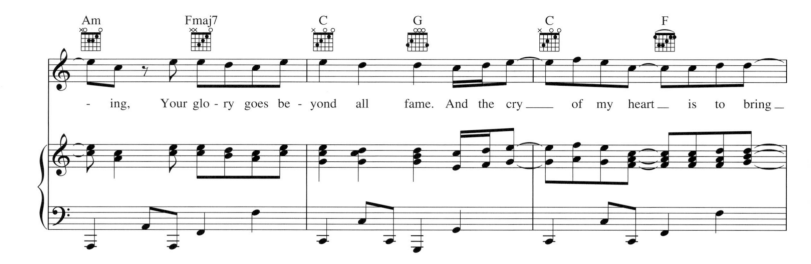

- ing, Your glo - ry goes be - yond all fame. And the cry___ of my heart___ is to bring___

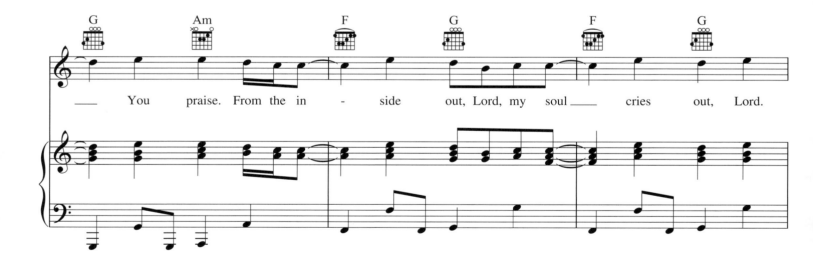

___ You praise. From the in - side out, Lord, my soul___ cries out, Lord.

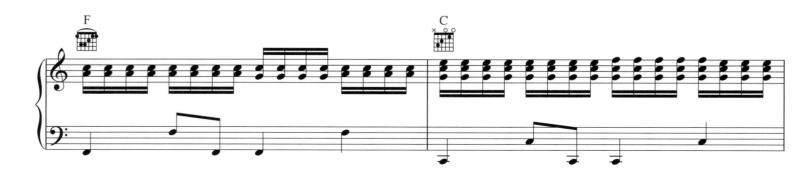

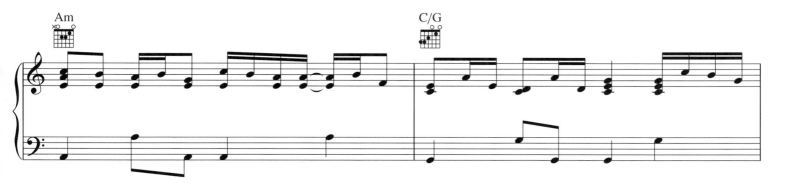

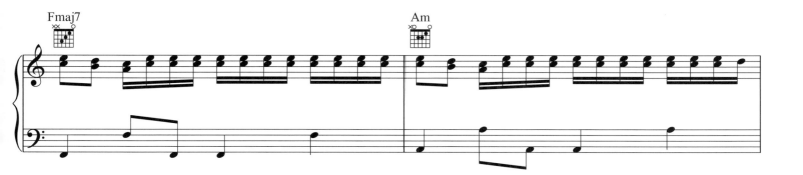

In my heart and my soul, ___ well, I give You con-trol. ___ Con-sume me from the

in - side out, Lord. Let jus - tice and praise ___ be - come my em - brace, ___

cresc. poco a poco

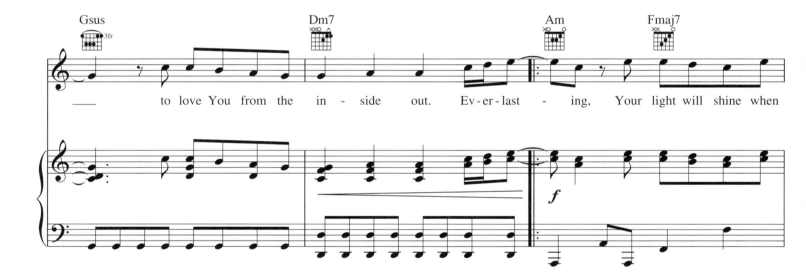

___ to love You from the in - side out. Ev - er - last - ing, Your light will shine when

all else fades. Nev - er - end - ing, Your glo - ry goes be - yond all fame. And the cry ___

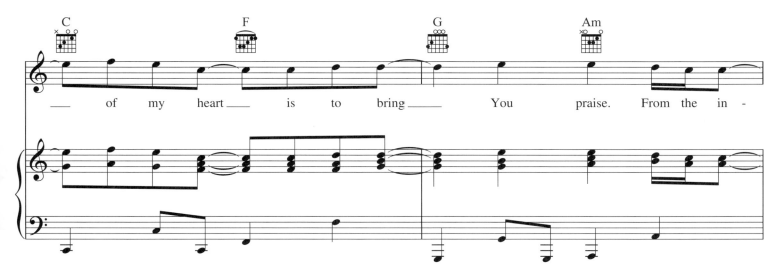

of my heart ___ is to bring ___ You praise. From the in -

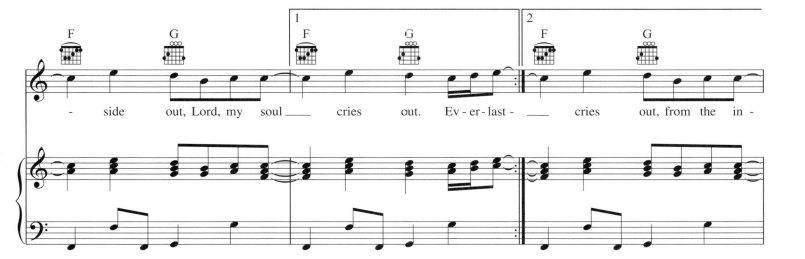

- side out, Lord, my soul ___ cries out. Ev - er - last - ___ cries out, from the in -

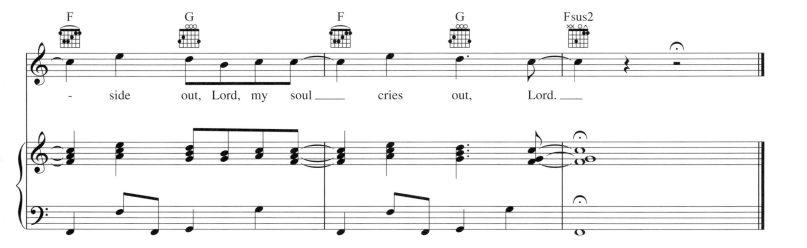

- side out, Lord, my soul ___ cries out, Lord. ___

GOD YOU REIGN

Words and Music by LINCOLN BREWSTER
and MIA FIELDES

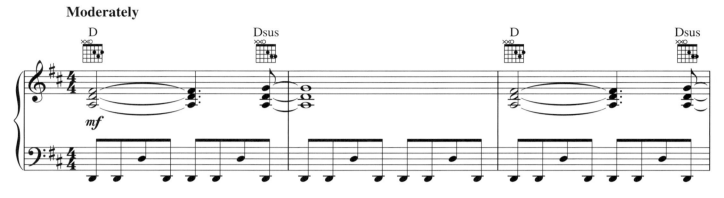

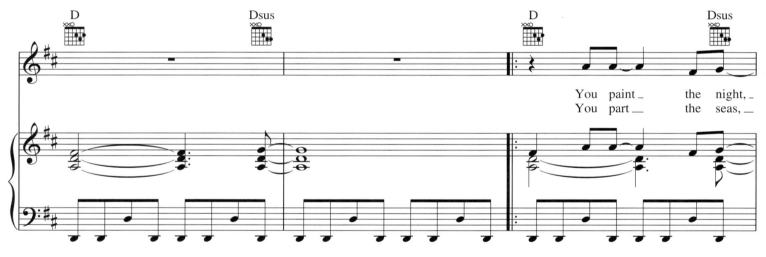

You paint ___ the night, ___
You part ___ the seas, ___

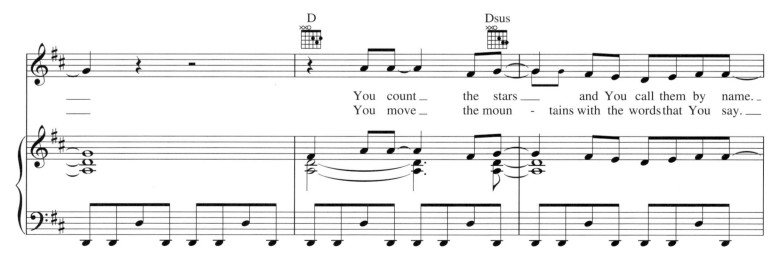

You count ___ the stars ___ and You call them by name. ___
You move ___ the moun - tains with the words that You say. ___

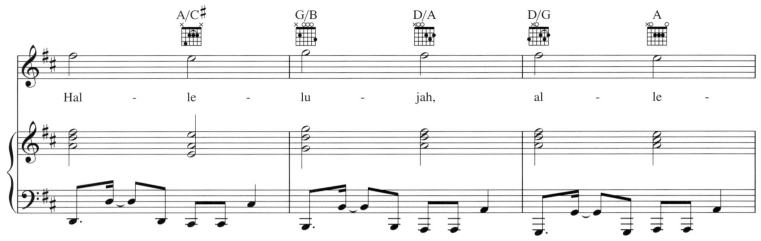

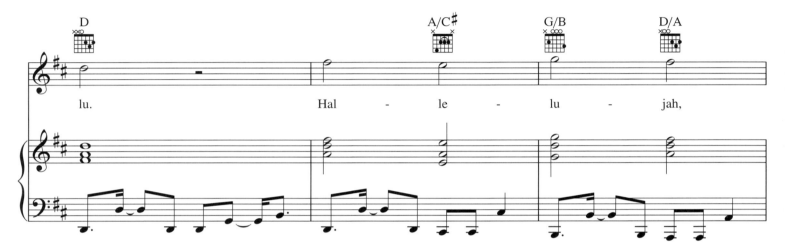

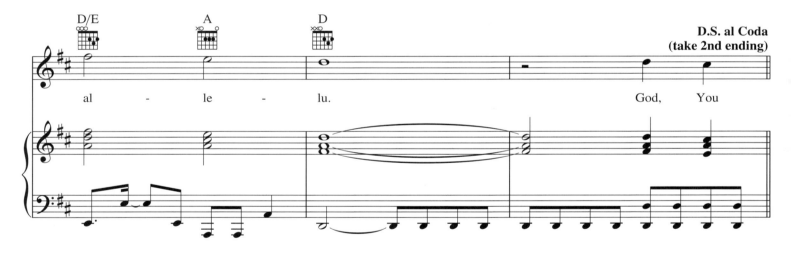

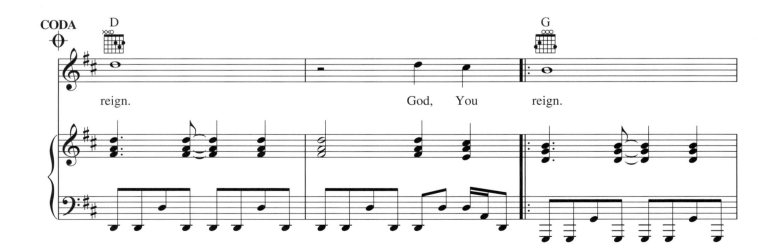

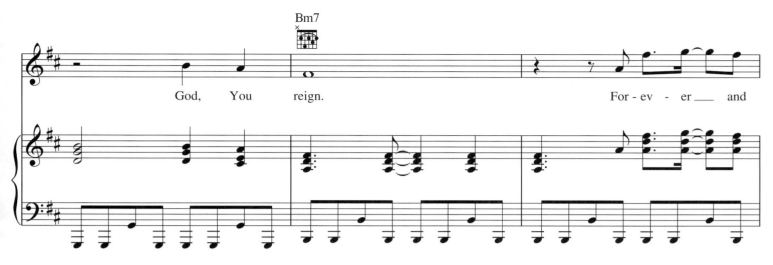

God, You reign. For - ev - er ___ and

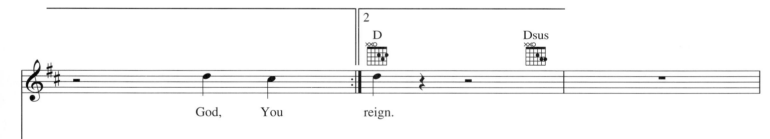

ev - er, God, You reign.

God, You reign.

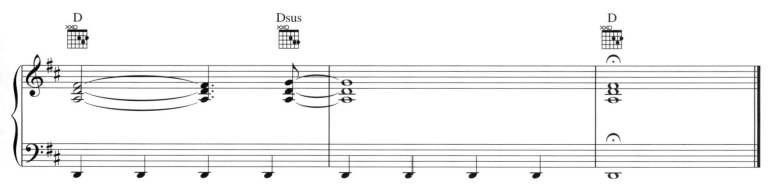

HEALER

Words and Music by
MIKE GUGLIELMUCCI

Moderately

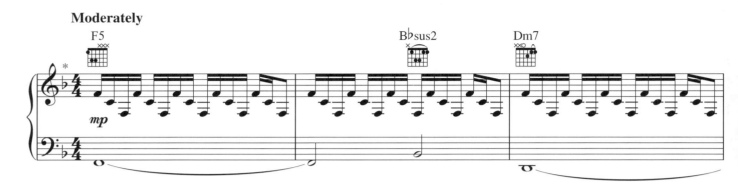

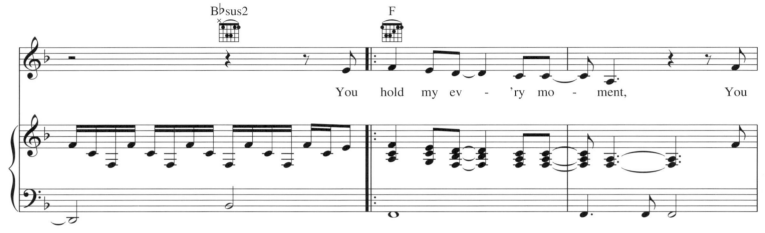

You hold my ev - 'ry mo - ment, You

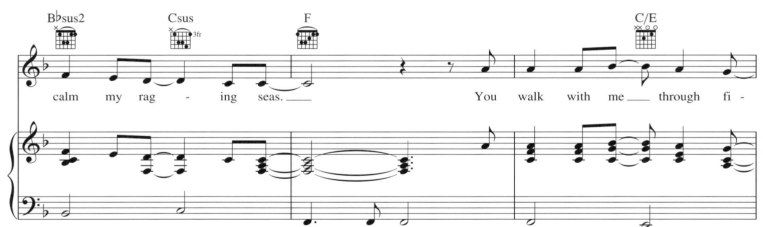

calm my rag - ing seas. ___ You walk with me ___ through fi -

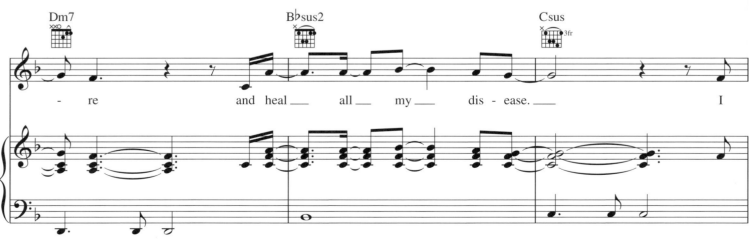

- re and heal ___ all ___ my ___ dis - ease. ___ I

* Recorded a half step higher.

trust in You, I trust in _____

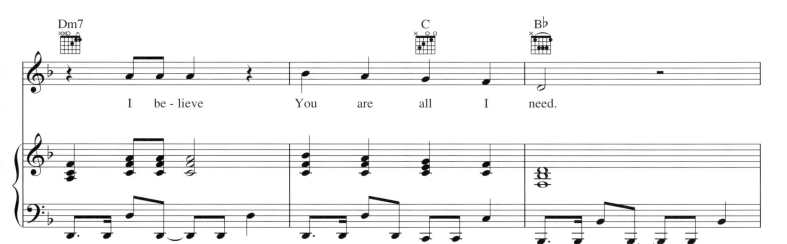

You. I be-lieve You're my heal-er.

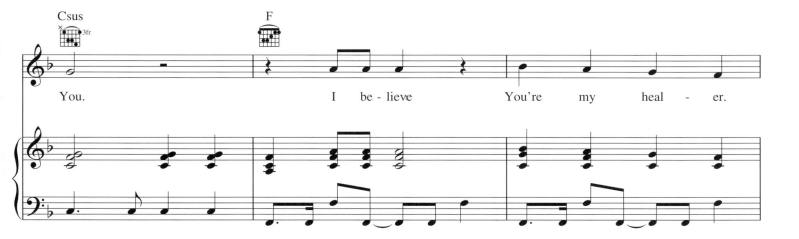

I be-lieve You are all I need.

I be-lieve. ___ I be-lieve You're my por-tion.

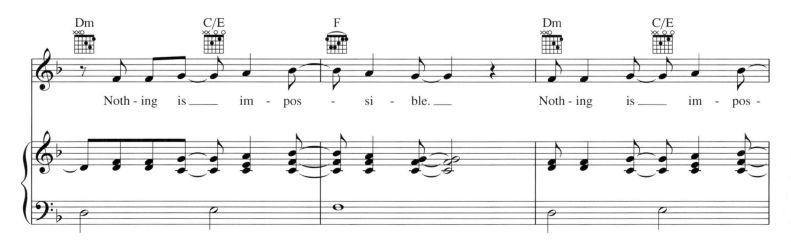

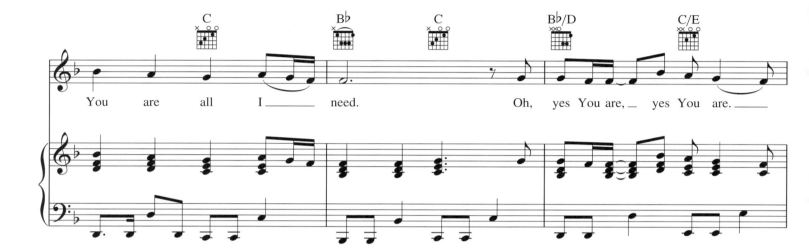

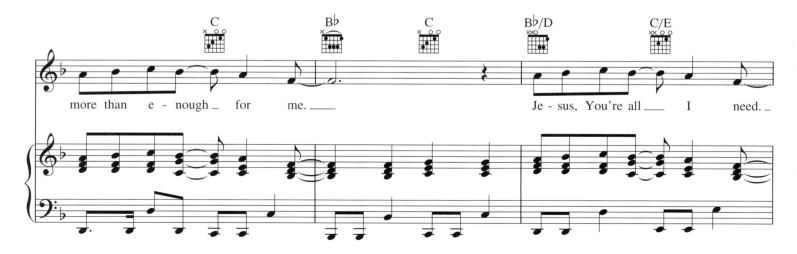

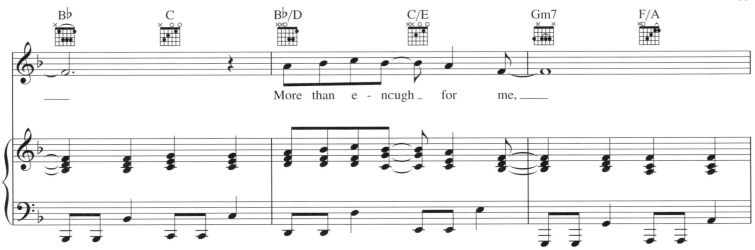

More than e-nough for me, ____

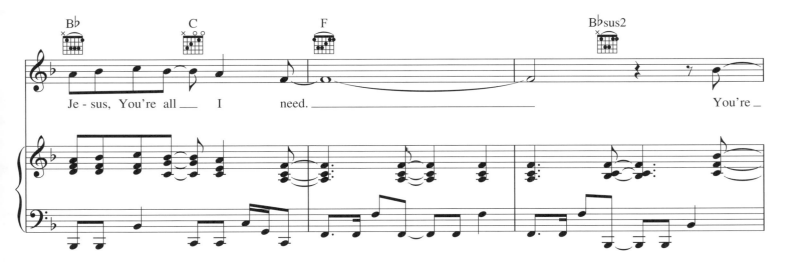

Je - sus, You're all ___ I need. _____ You're _

____ my heal - er. ____

rit.

HERE I AM TO WORSHIP

Words and Music by
TIM HUGHES

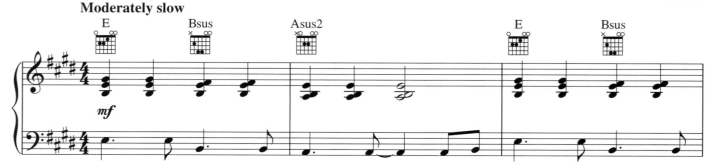

Light of the World, You stepped down in-to dark - ness,
King of all days, oh, so high - ly ex - alt - ed,

o - pened my eyes, let me ____ see. ____
glo - rious in heav - en a - bove. ____

Beau - ty that made this ____
Hum - bly You came to the

heart a - dore ____ You, hope of a life spent with ____ You. ____
earth You cre - at - ed, all for love's sake be - came ____ poor. ____

Here I am to wor-ship, here I am to bow down, here I am to

say that You're my God. ___ You're al-to-geth-er love-ly, al-to-geth-er

wor-thy, al-to-geth-er won-der-ful to me. ___

To Coda ⊕

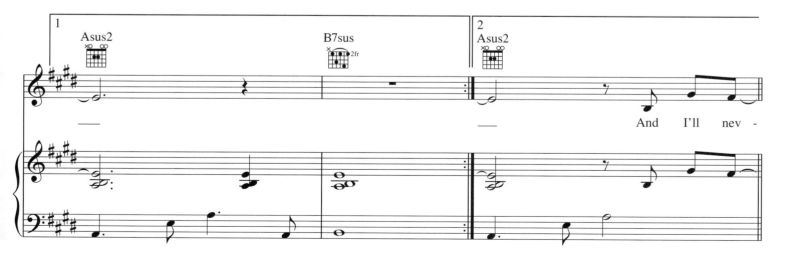

And I'll nev-

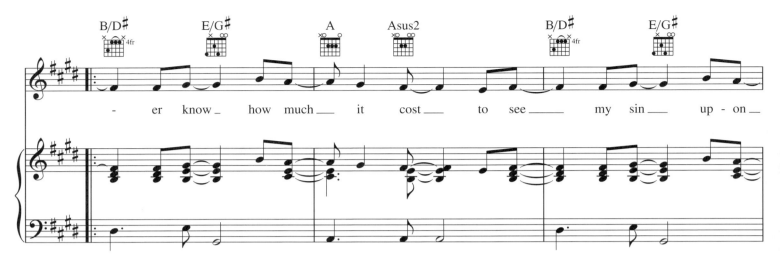

-er know_ how much_ it cost_ to see_ my sin_ up - on_

_ that cross._ And I'll nev- _ that cross._ Here I am to

D.S. al Coda

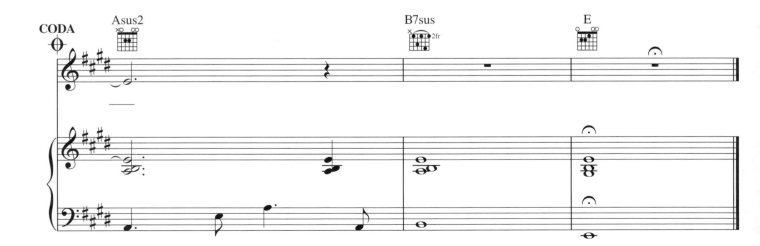

CODA

HOW HE LOVES

Words and Music by
JOHN MARK McMILLAN

Slowly, in 2

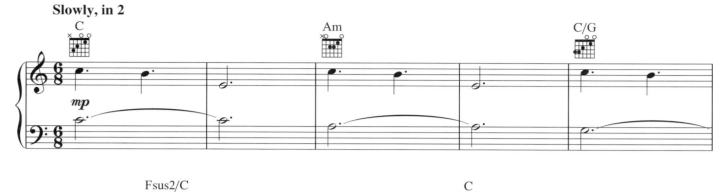

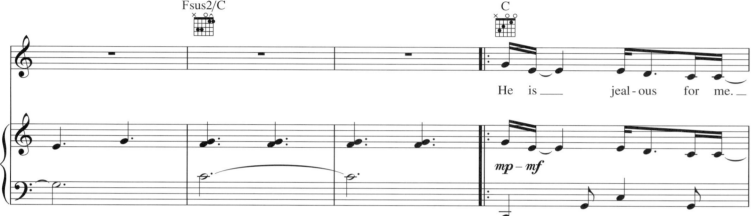

He is ___ jeal-ous for me. ___

___ Loves like a hur - ri - cane; I am a tree, ___

bend - ing be - neath ___ the weight of His wind and ___ mer - cy. ___

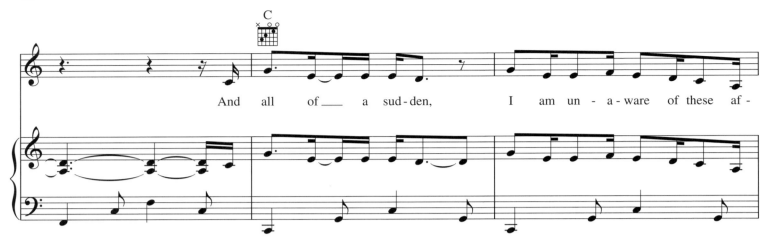

And all of ___ a sud-den, I am un-a-ware of these af-

flic - tions e - clipsed by ___ glo - ry, ___ and I

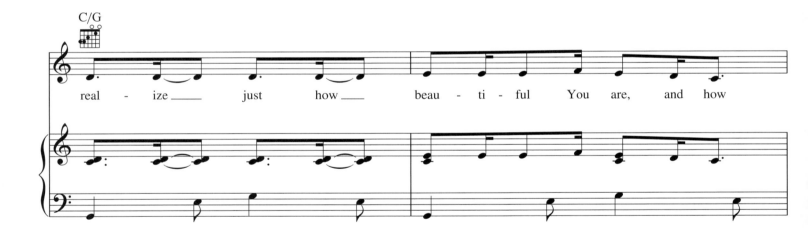

real - ize ___ just how ___ beau - ti - ful You are, and how

great Your af - fec - tions are ___ for me. ___ And oh,

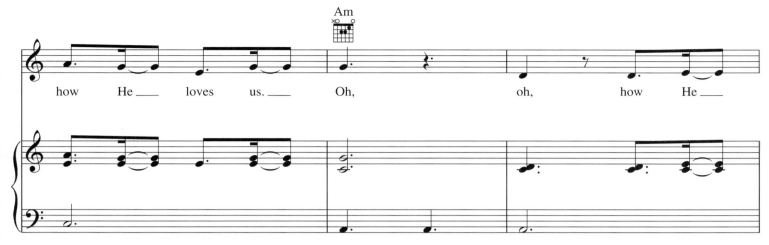

how He ___ loves us. ___ Oh, oh, how He ___

loves ___ us, ___ how He ___ loves us _____ all.

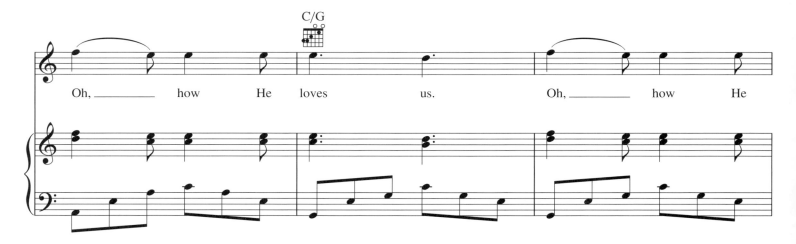

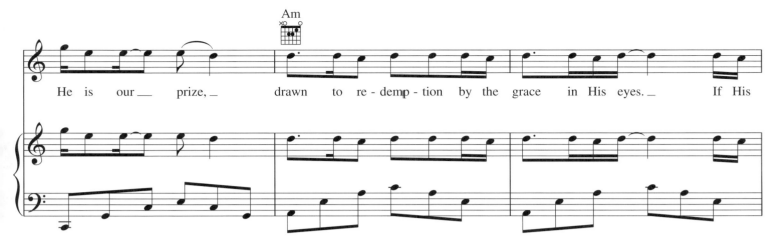

He is our __ prize, __ drawn to re-demp-tion by the grace in His eyes. __ If His

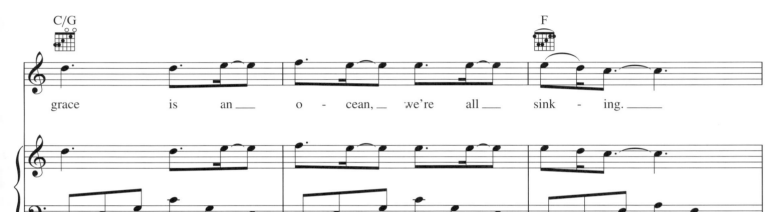

grace is an __ o-cean, __ we're all __ sink - ing. ____

And heav-en meets __ earth like an un-fore-seen kiss, and my

heart turns __ vio-lent-ly in-side of my chest. I don't have __ time to main -

tain these re - grets __ when I think a - bout the way __ that He

loves us. Oh, __ how He loves us.

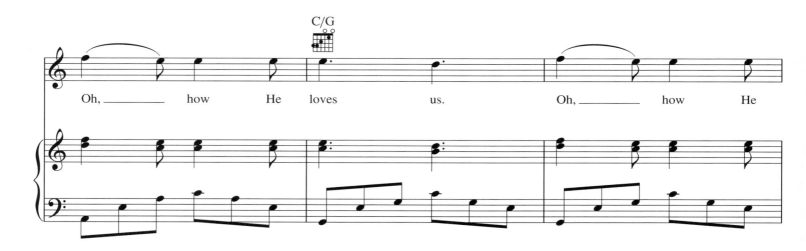

Oh, __ how He loves us. Oh, __ how He

loves. __ Yeah, He

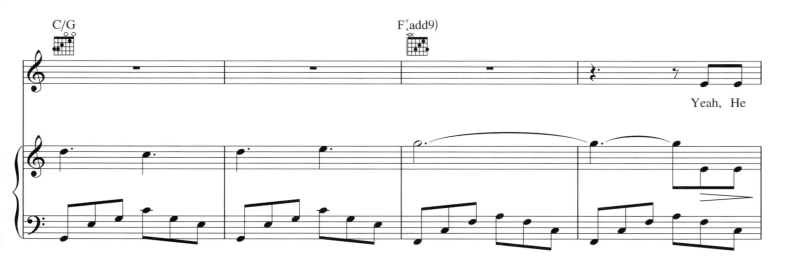

Yeah, He

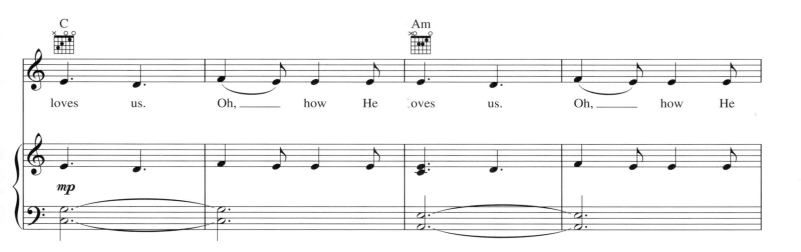

loves us. Oh, _____ how He loves us. Oh, _____ how He

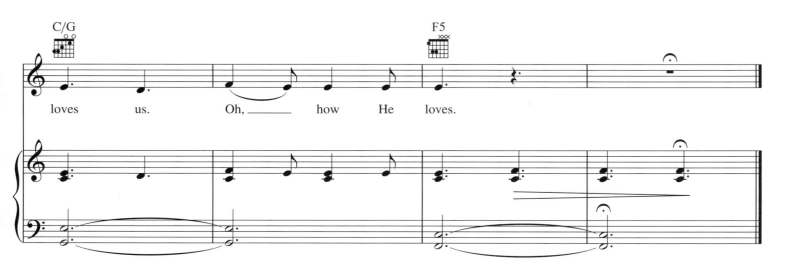

loves us. Oh, _____ how He loves.

HOLY IS THE LORD

Words and Music by CHRIS TOMLIN
and LOUIE GIGLIO

With praise

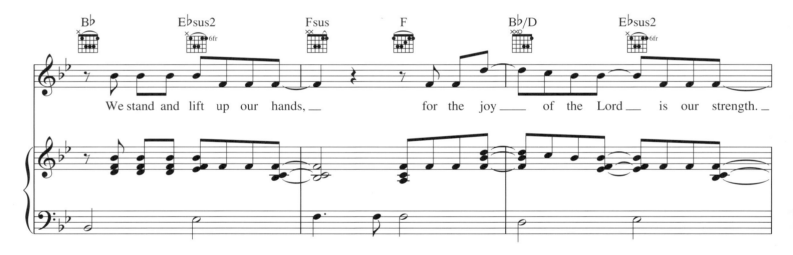

We stand and lift up our hands, ___ for the joy ___ of the Lord ___ is our strength. ___

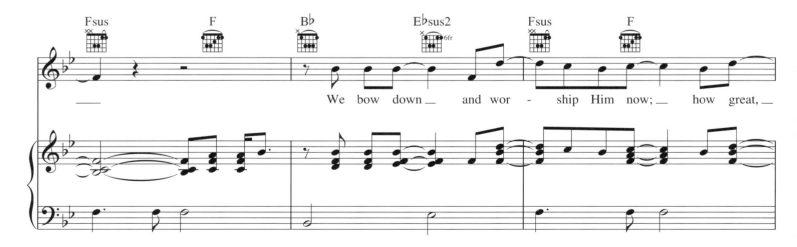

___ We bow down ___ and wor - ship Him now; ___ how great, ___

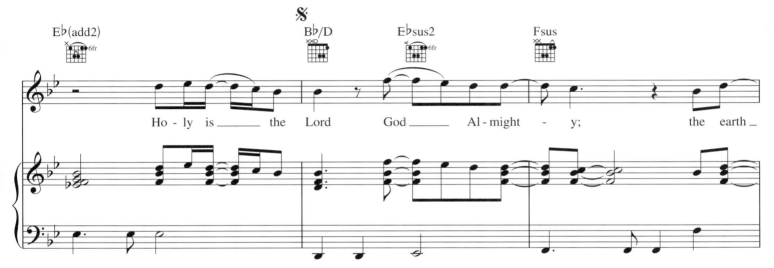

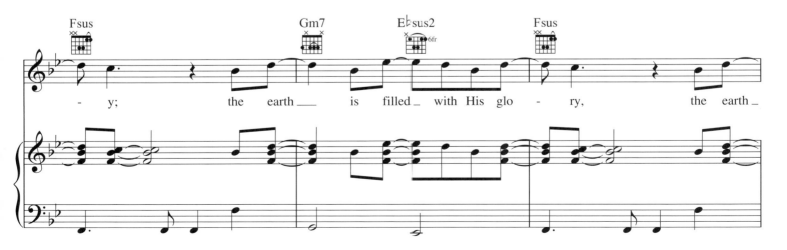

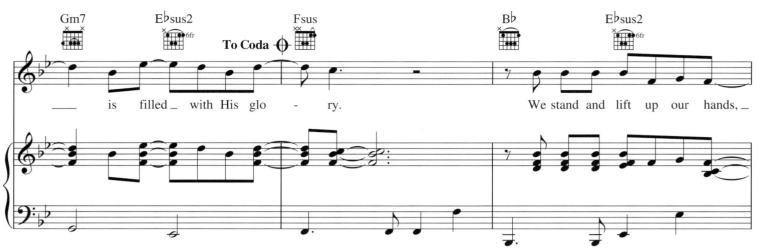

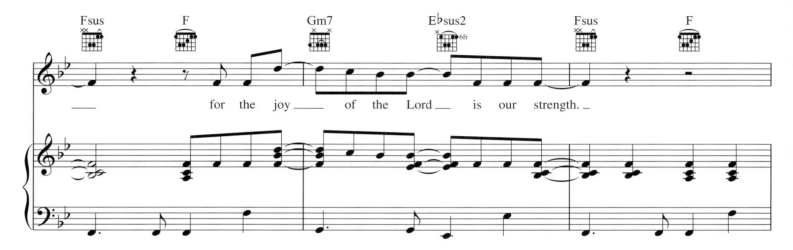

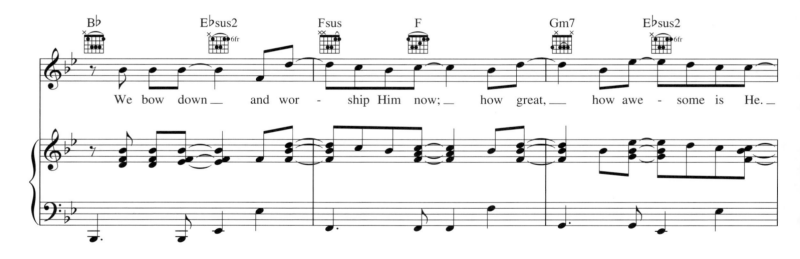

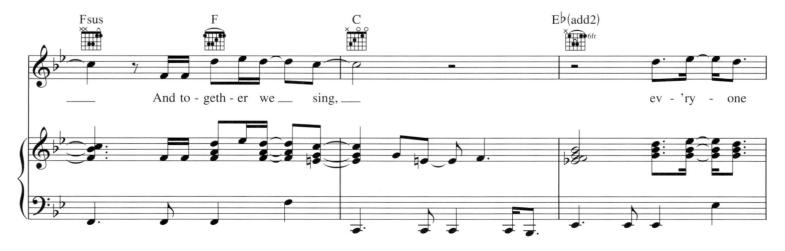

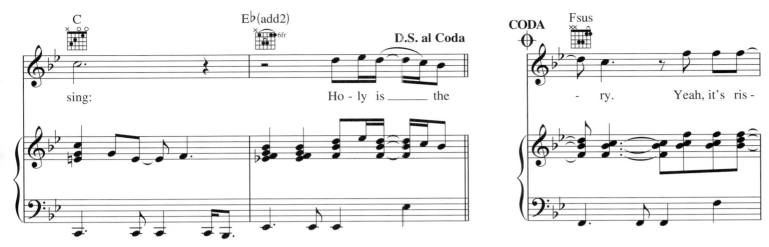

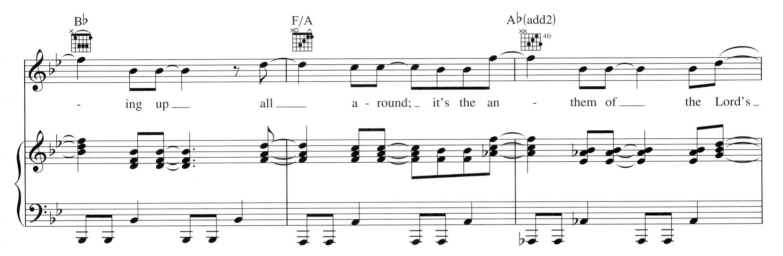

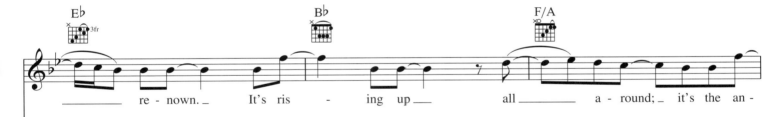

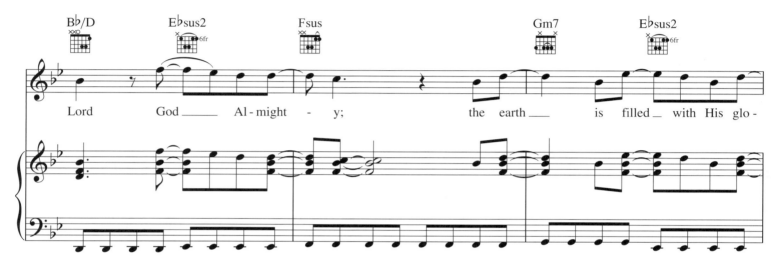

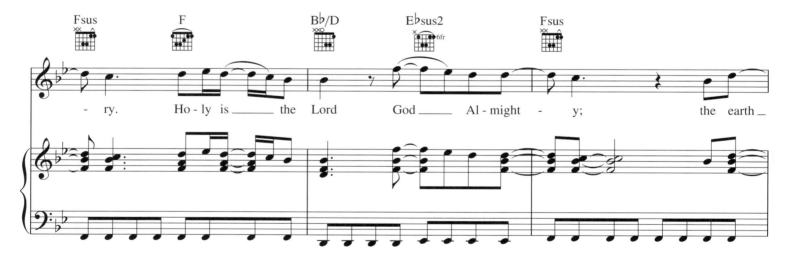

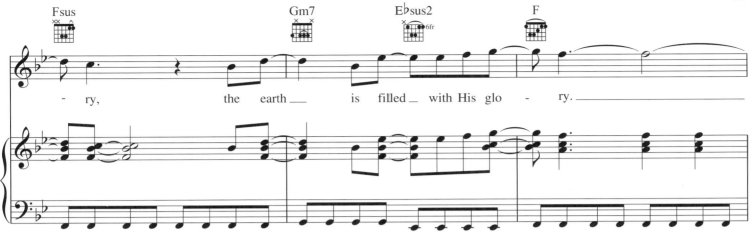

- ry, the earth is filled with His glo - ry.

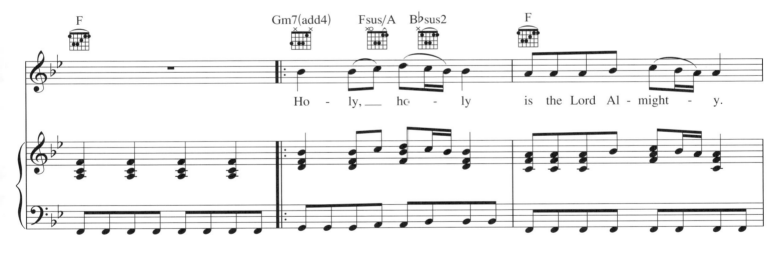

Ho - ly, ho - ly is the Lord Al - might - y.

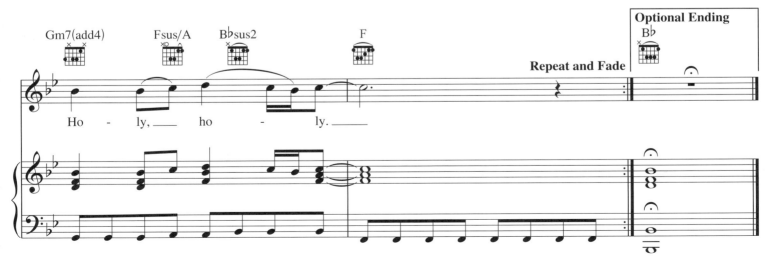

Ho - ly, ho - ly.

Optional Ending

Repeat and Fade

HOSANNA

Words and Music by
BROOKE FRASER

Moderately

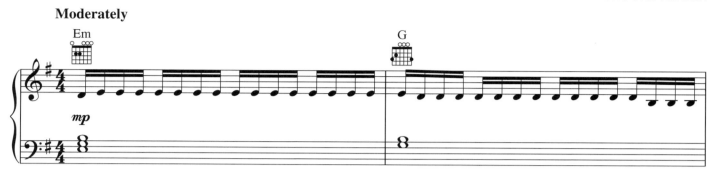

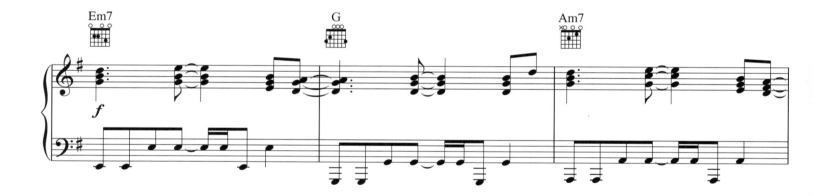

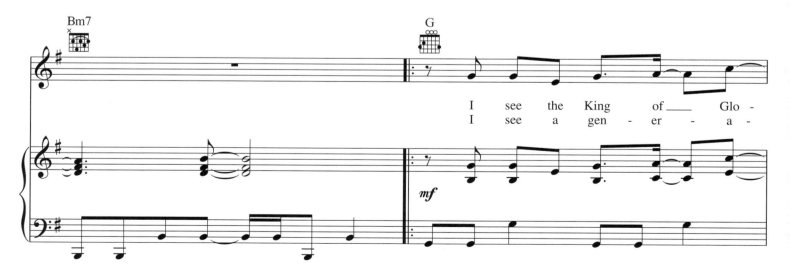

I see the King of ___ Glo-
I see a gen - er - a-

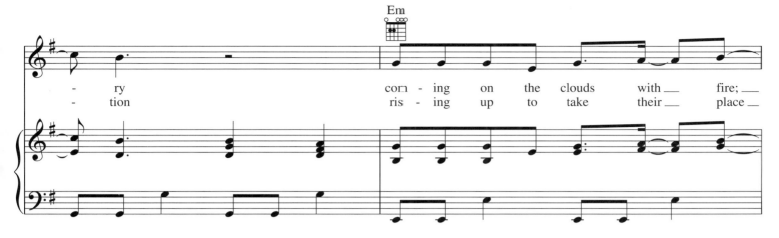

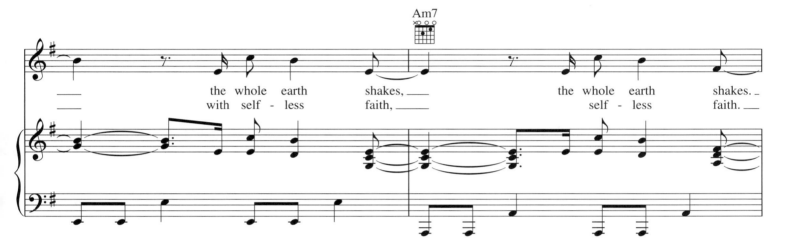

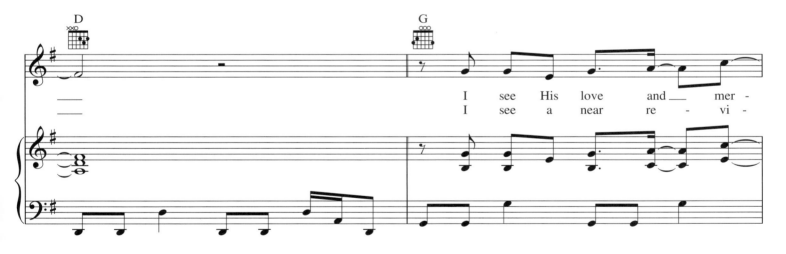

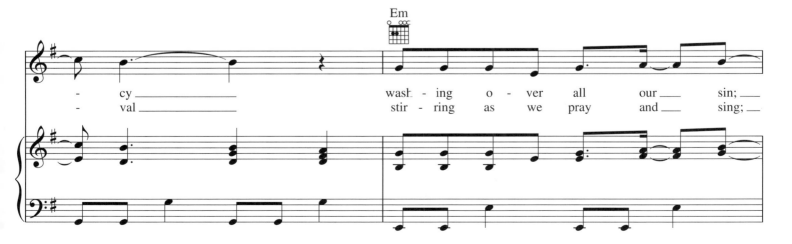

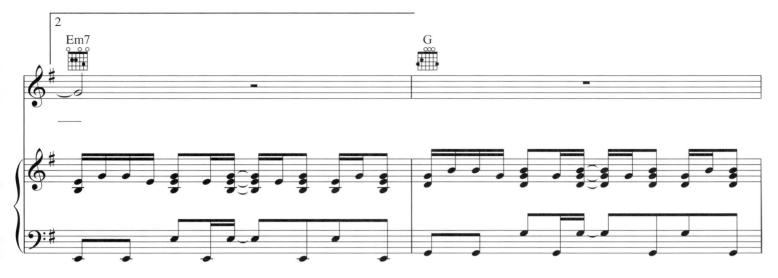

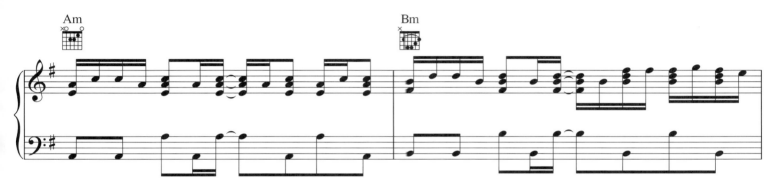

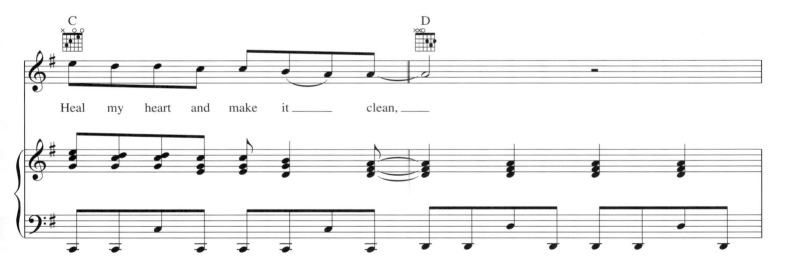

Heal my heart and make it ____ clean, ____

o - pen up my eyes to the things un - seen. ____

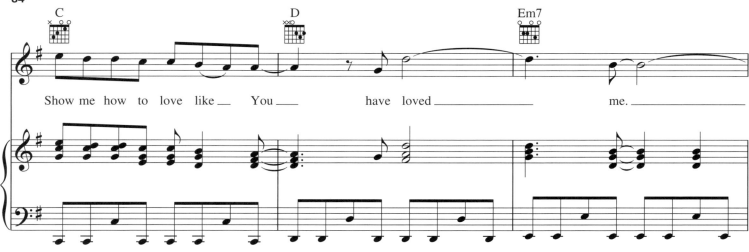

Show me how to love like ___ You ___ have loved _____ me. _____

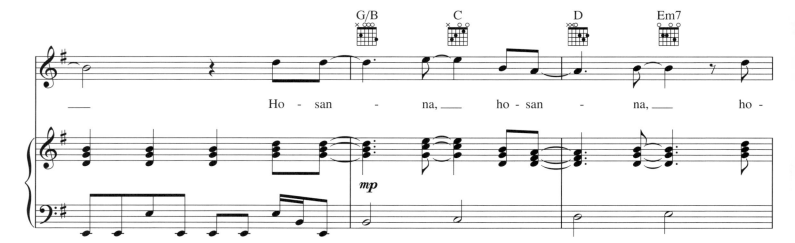

___ Ho - san - na, ___ ho - san - na, ___ ho -

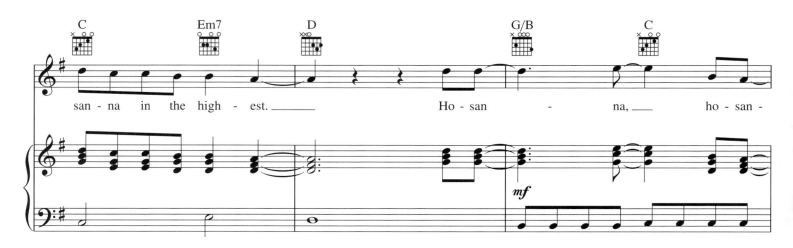

san - na in the high - est. _____ Ho - san ___ na, ___ ho - san -

D.S. al Coda

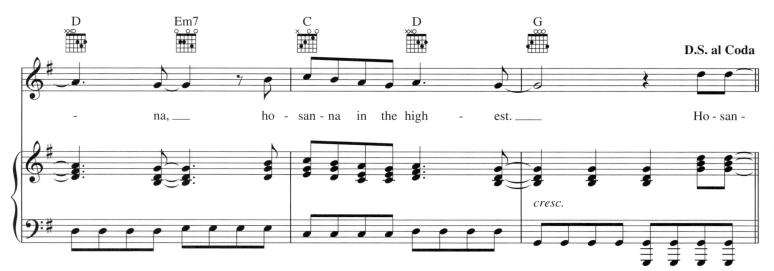

- na, ___ ho - san - na in the high - est. ___ Ho - san -

cresc.

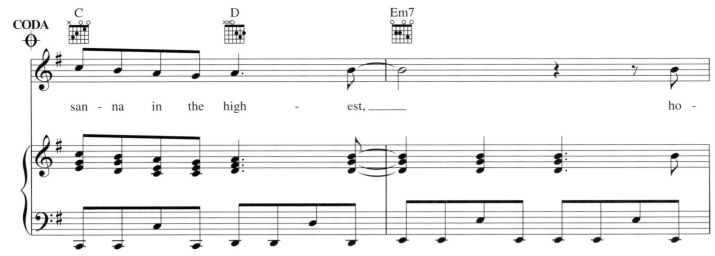

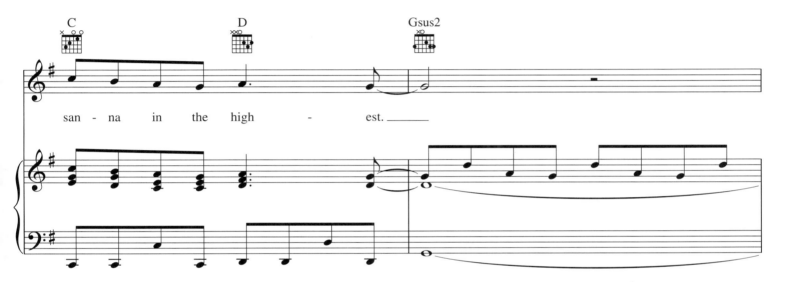

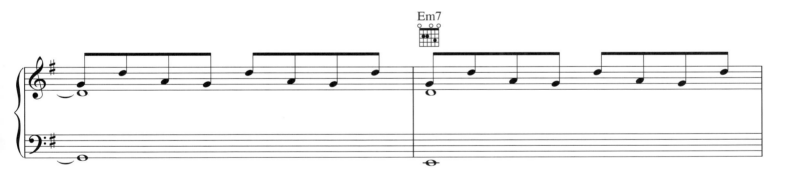

HOSANNA
(Praise Is Rising)

Words and Music by PAUL BALOCHE
and BRENTON BROWN

With a driving beat

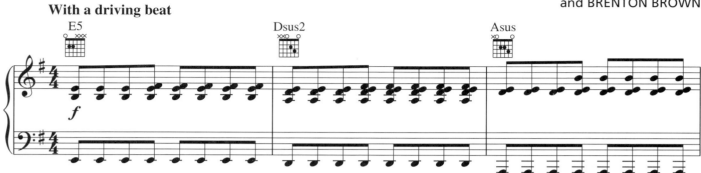

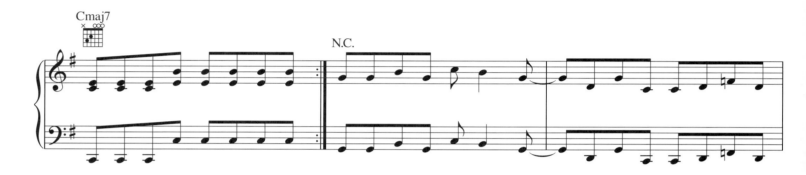

Praise ___ is
Hear ___ the

ris - ing,   eyes ___ are   turn - ing ___ to You, ___
sound ___ of   hearts ___ re - turn - ing ___ to You, ___

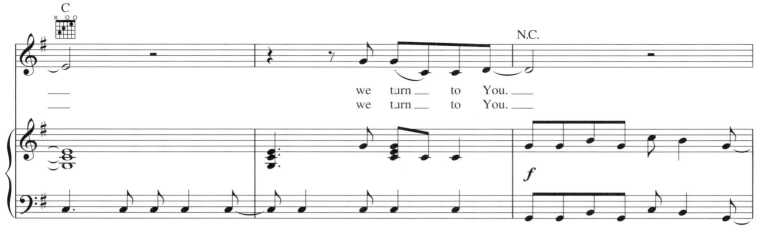

we turn to You.
we turn to You.

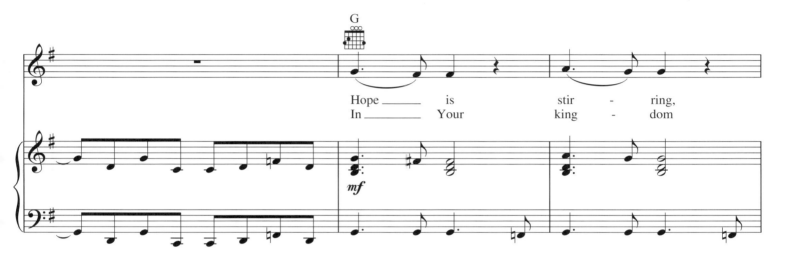

Hope is stir - ring,
In Your king - dom

hearts are yearn - ing for You,
bro - ken lives are re - newed;

we long for You.
You make us new.

'Cause when we see

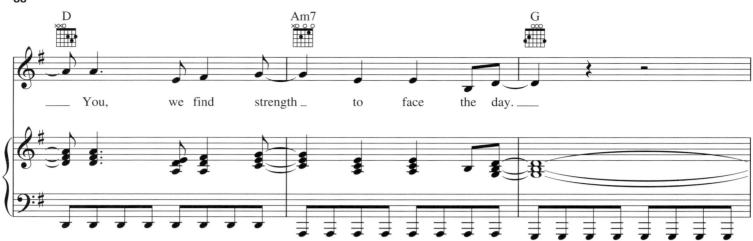

You, we find strength to face the day.

In Your pres - ence, all our fears are washed a - way,

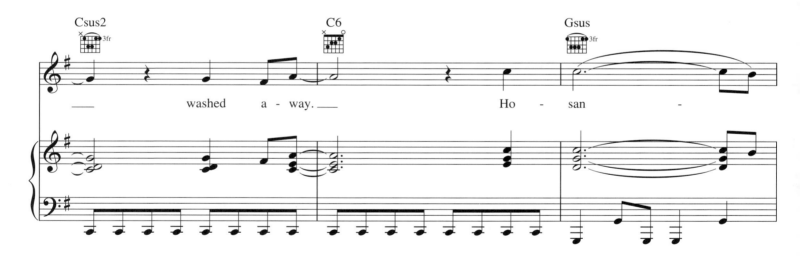

washed a - way. Ho - san -

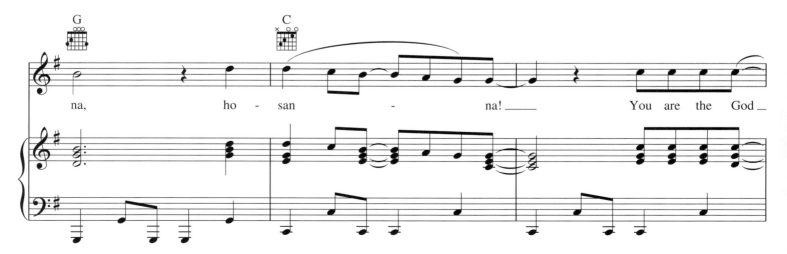

na, ho - san - na! You are the God

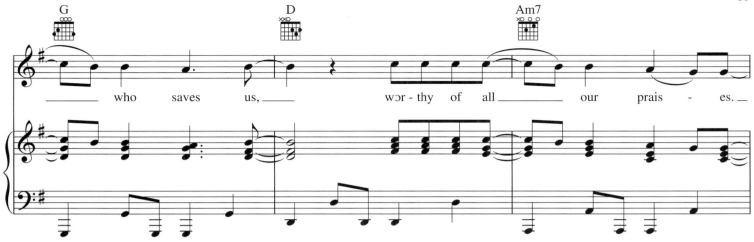

who saves us, _____ wor-thy of all _____ our prais - es. ____

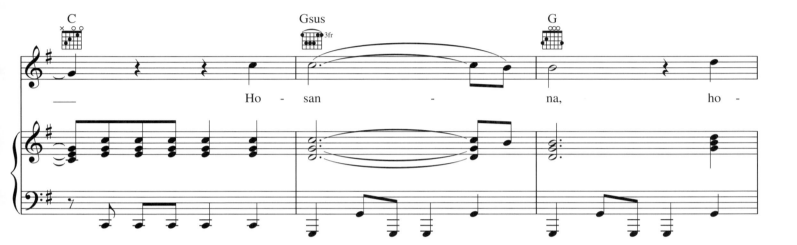

Ho - san - na, _____ ho -

san - na! _____ Come, have Your way ____

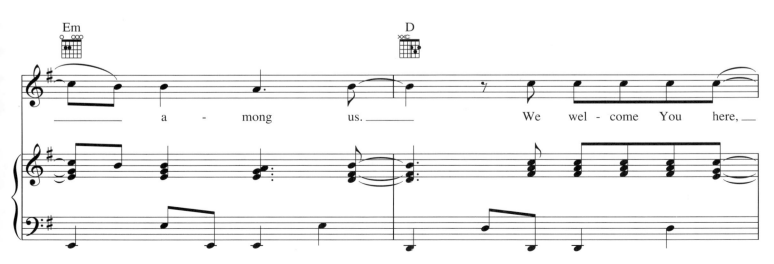

____ a - mong us. ____ We wel - come You here, ____

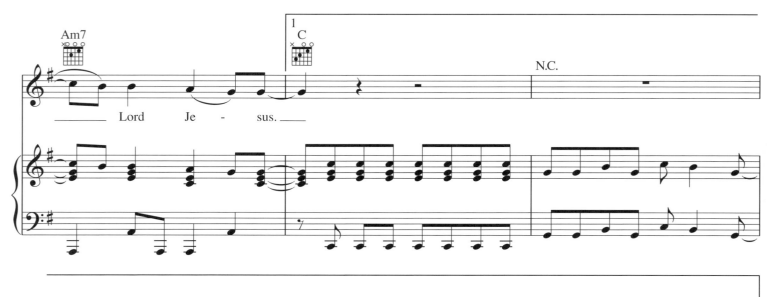

Lord Je - sus.

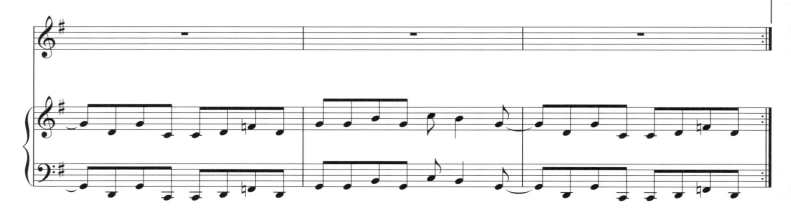

Ho - san - na!

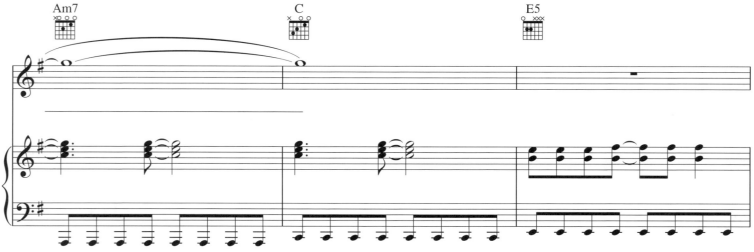

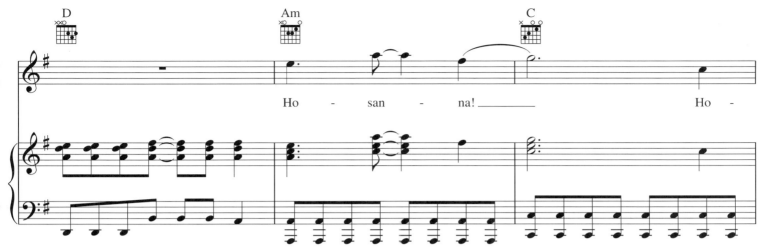

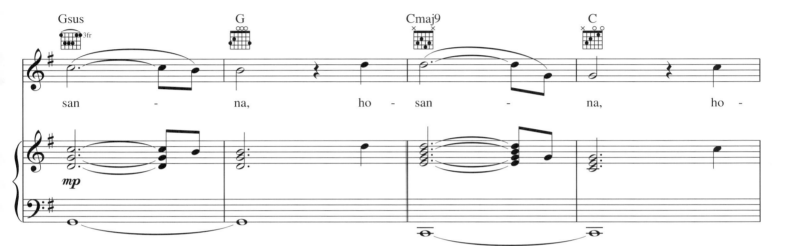

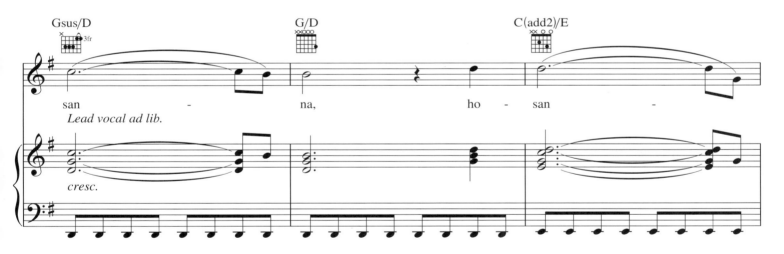

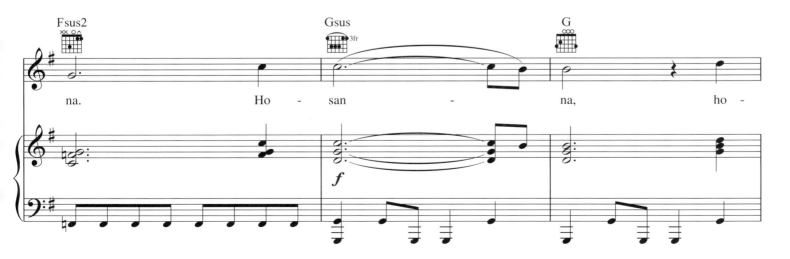

san - na! _____ Come, have Your way _____

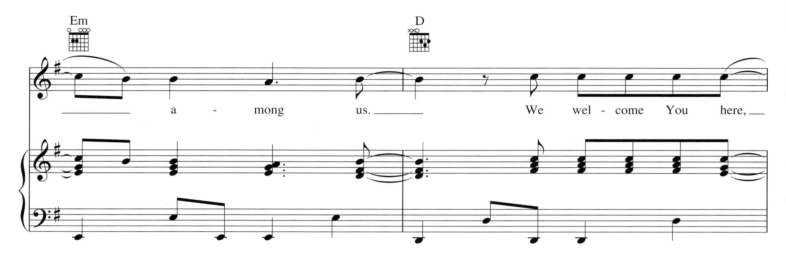

_____ a - mong us. _____ We wel - come You here, _____

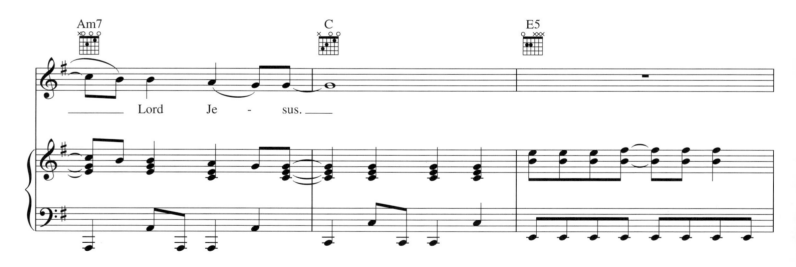

_____ Lord Je - sus. _____

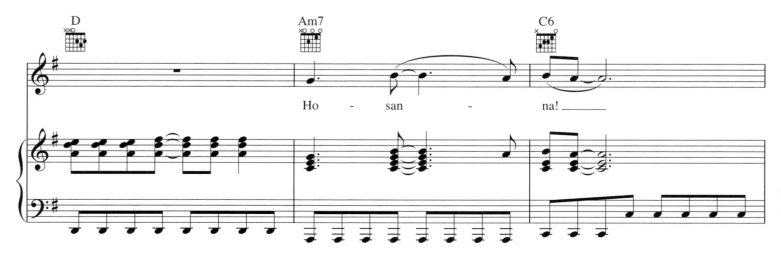

Ho - san - na! _____

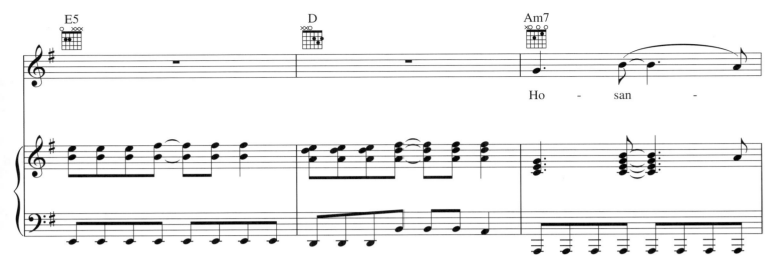

HOW GREAT IS OUR GOD

Words and Music by CHRIS TOMLIN,
JESSE REEVES and ED CASH

With praise

The splen-dor of ___ a King, ___
age to age ___ He stands, ___ and

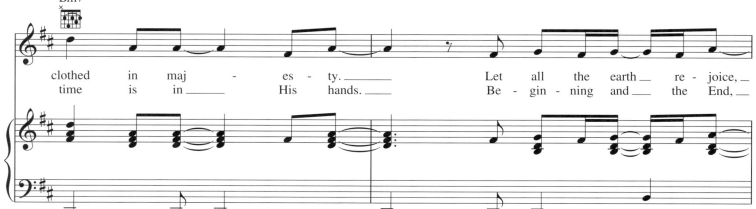

clothed in maj - es - ty. ___ Let all the earth ___ re - joice, ___
time is in ___ His hands. ___ Be - gin - ning and ___ the End, ___

___ all the earth ___ re - joice. ___ He wraps ___ Him - self ___ in light, ___
___ Be - gin - ning and ___ the End. ___ The God - head, Three ___ in One, ___

* Recorded a half step lower.

How great ___ is our God! ___

Sing with me: ___ How great ___ is our God! ___

___ And all ___ will see how great, how great ___ is our God! ___

How great ___ ___

HUNGRY
(Falling on My Knees)

Words and Music by
KATHRYN SCOTT

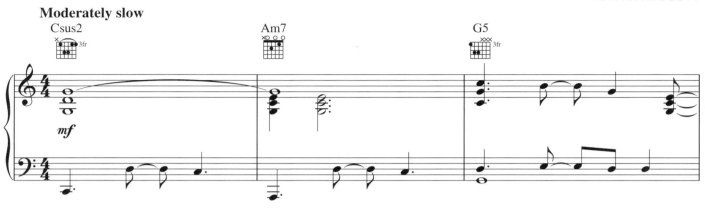

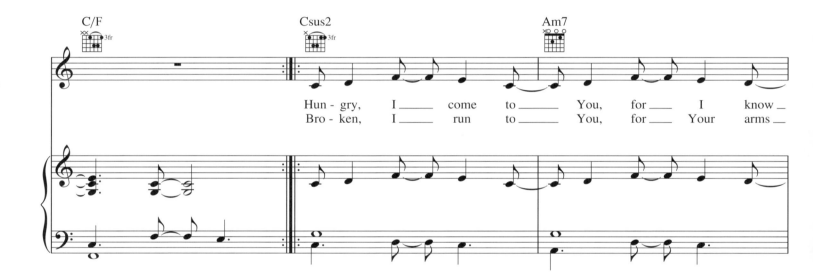

Hun - gry, I come to You, for I know
Bro - ken, I run to You, for Your arms

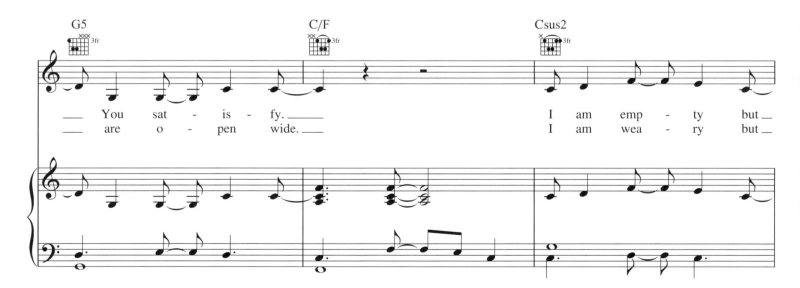

You sat - is - fy. I am emp - ty but
are o - pen wide. I am wea - ry but

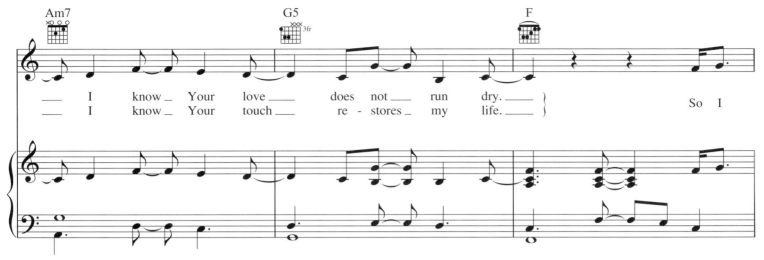

I know Your love does not run dry. So I
I know Your touch re-stores my life.

wait for You. So I wait for You.

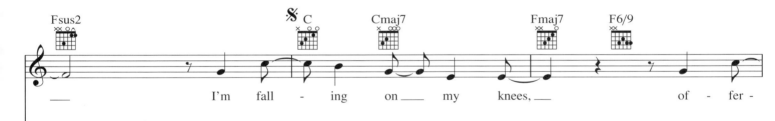

I'm fall-ing on my knees, of-fer-

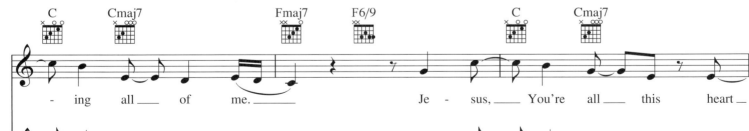

-ing all of me. Je-sus, You're all this heart

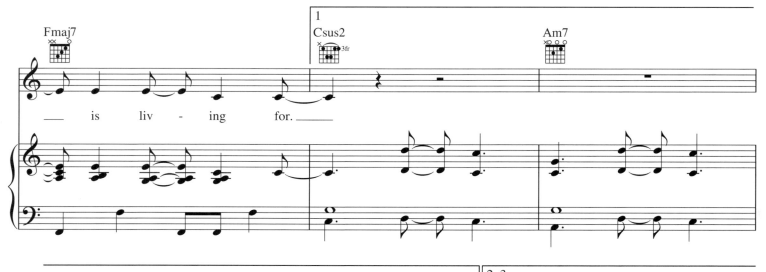

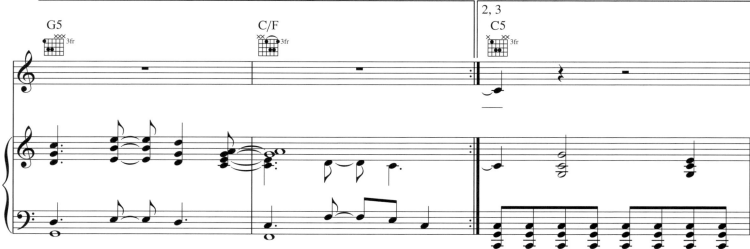

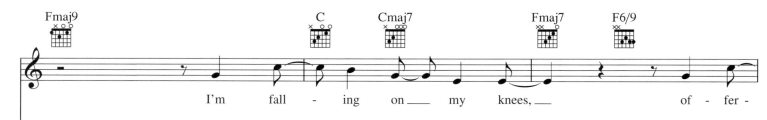

I'm fall - ing on ___ my knees, ___ of - fer -

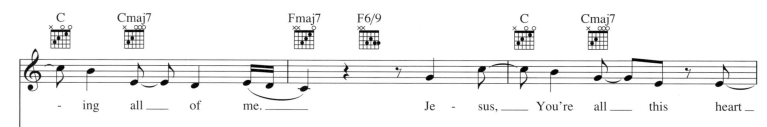

- ing all ___ of me. ___ Je - sus, ___ You're all ___ this heart ___

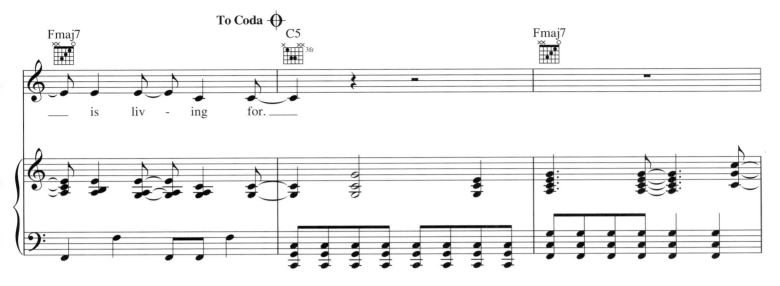

is liv - ing for.

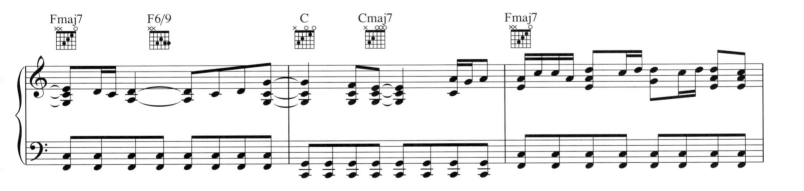

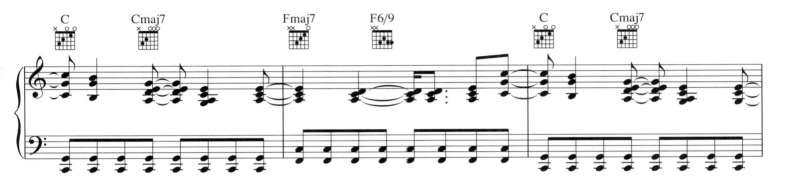

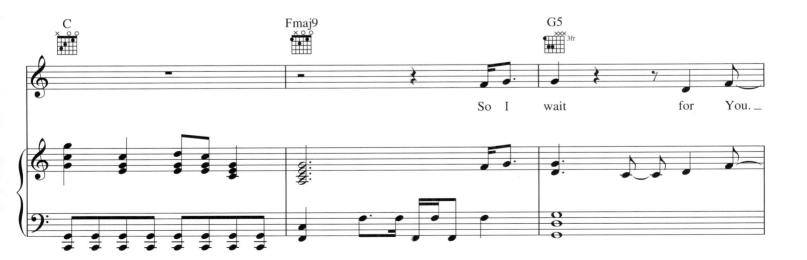

So I wait for You.

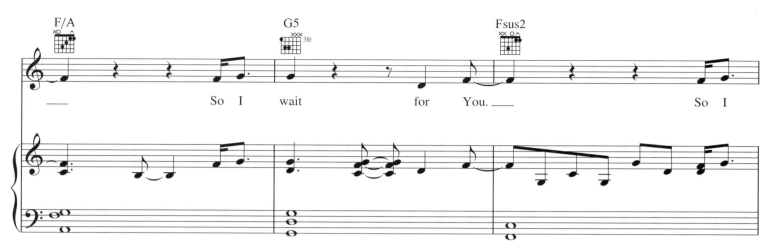

So I wait for You. _____ So I

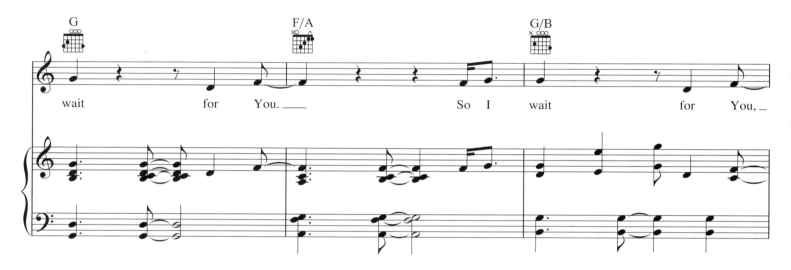

wait for You. _____ So I wait for You, _

D.S. al Coda
(take 2nd ending)

_____ and I'm fall -

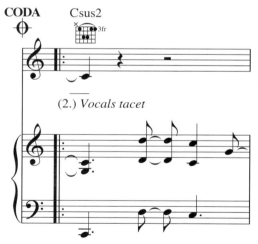

CODA

(2.) *Vocals tacet*

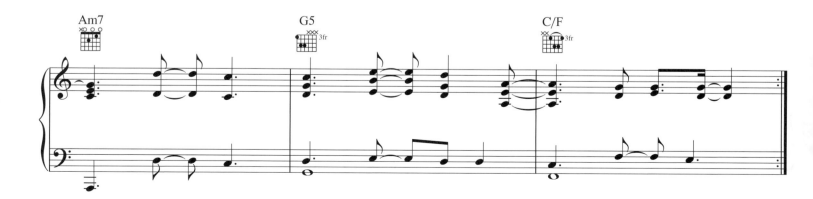

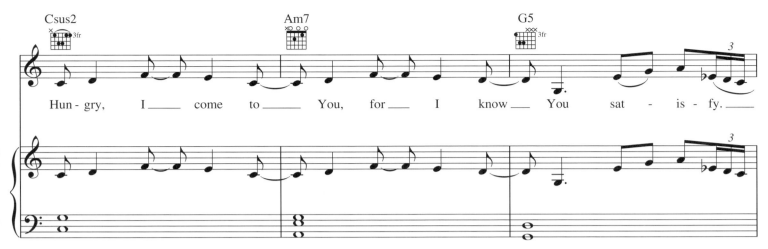

Hun - gry, I ___ come to ___ You, for ___ I know ___ You sat - is - fy. ___

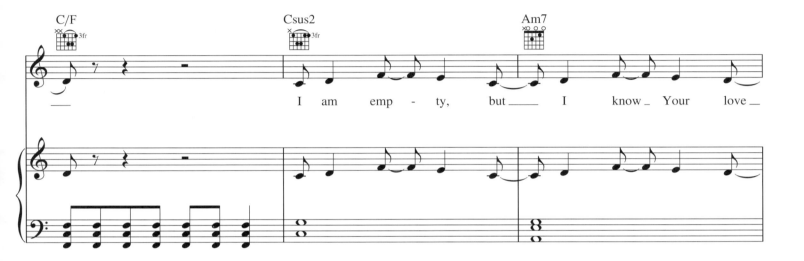

___ I am emp - ty, but ___ I know ___ Your love ___

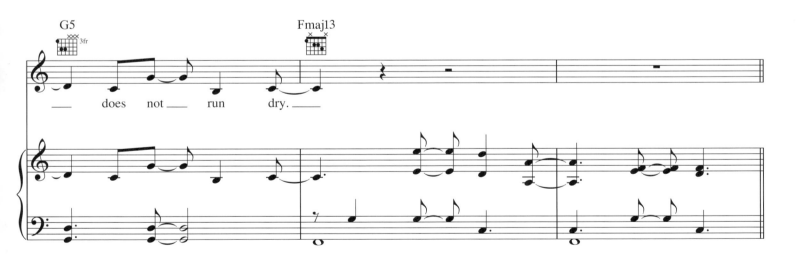

___ does not ___ run dry. ___

Optional Ending

Repeat ad lib. and Fade

I AM FREE

Words and Music by
JON EGAN

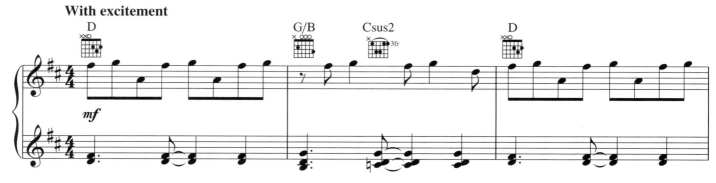

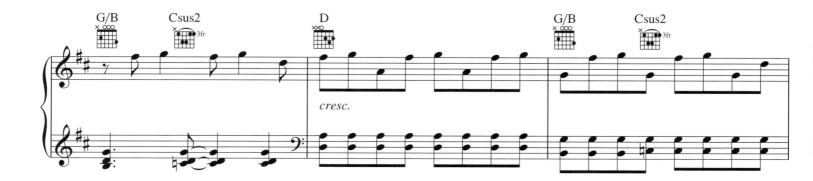

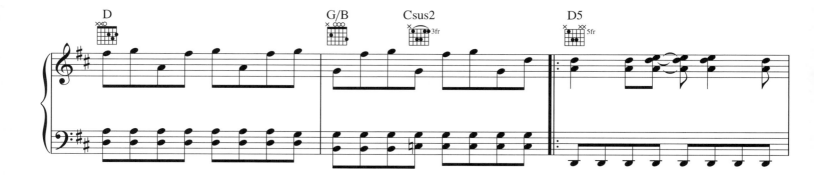

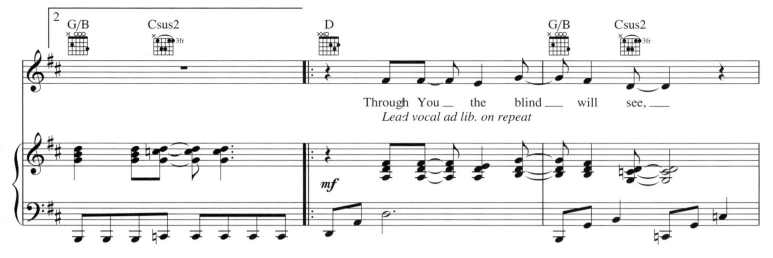

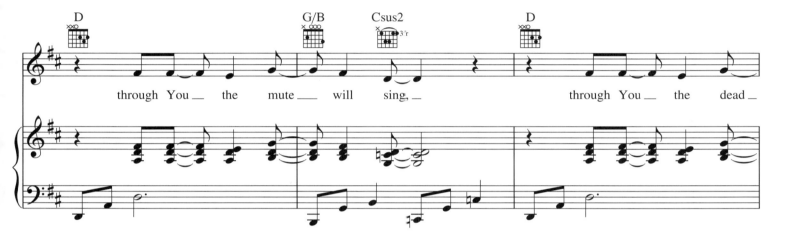

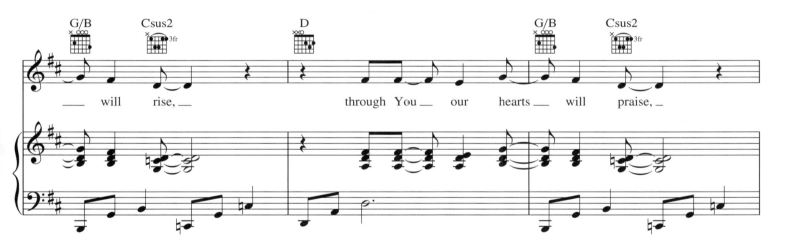

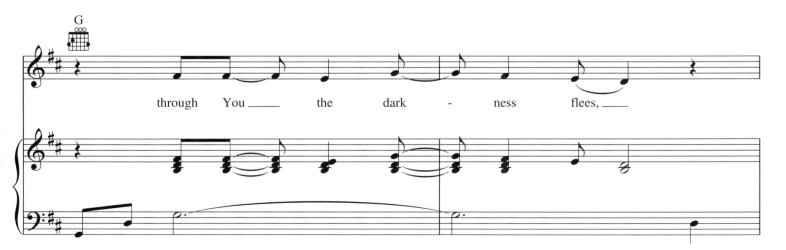

through You my heart screams, "I am free!

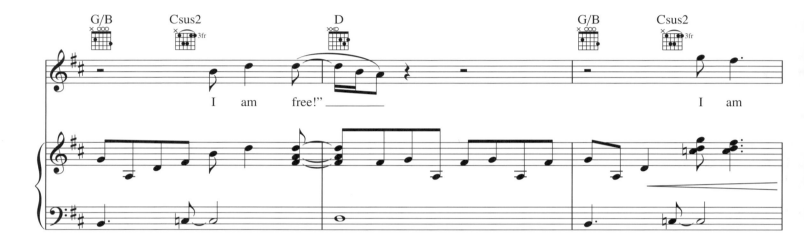

I am free!" I am

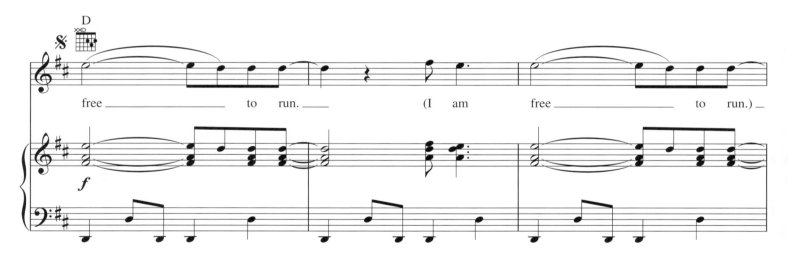

free to run. (I am free to run.)

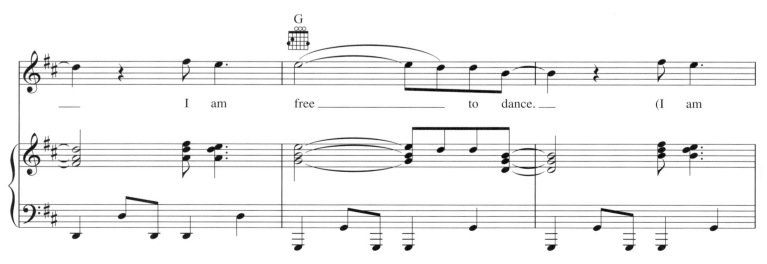

I am free to dance. (I am

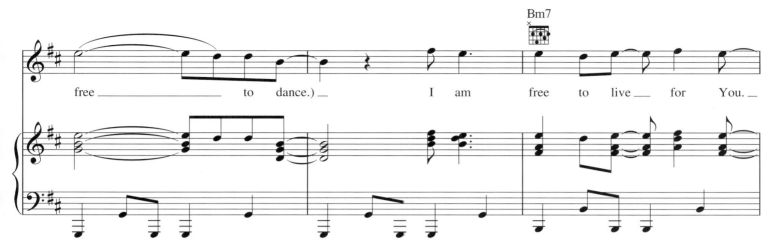

free _____ to dance.) __   I am   free   to live __ for You. __

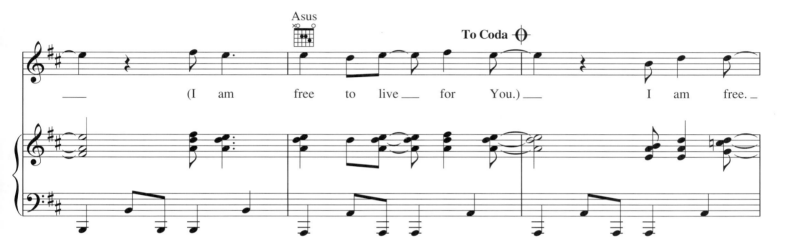

__   (I am   free   to live __ for   You.) __   I am   free. __

__   (I am   free.) __   I am   free. __   (I am   free.) __

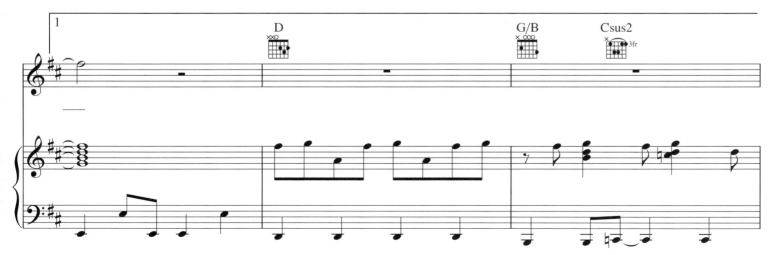

D.S. al Coda

— I am

— I am free, ___ (I am free.) ___ I ___ am free. ___

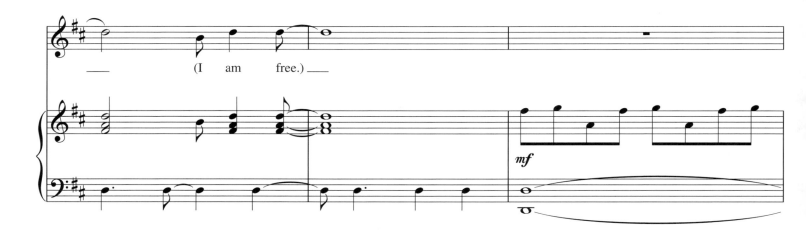

— (I am free.) ___

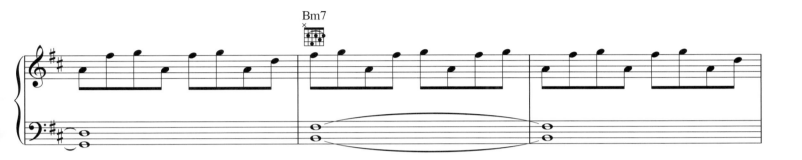

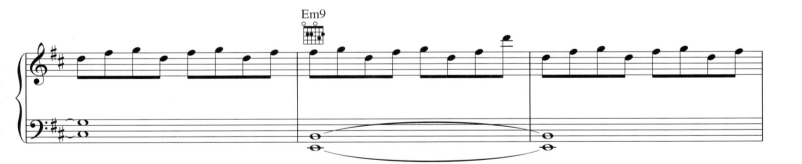

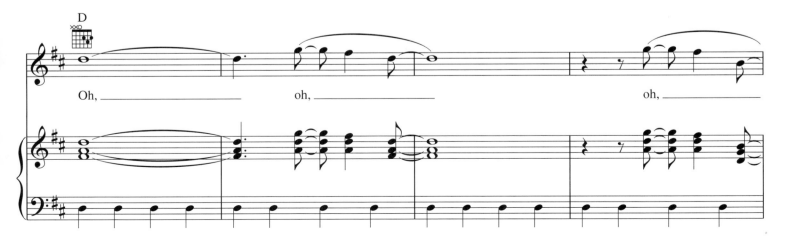

Oh, _____ oh, _____ oh, _____

oh, _____ oh,

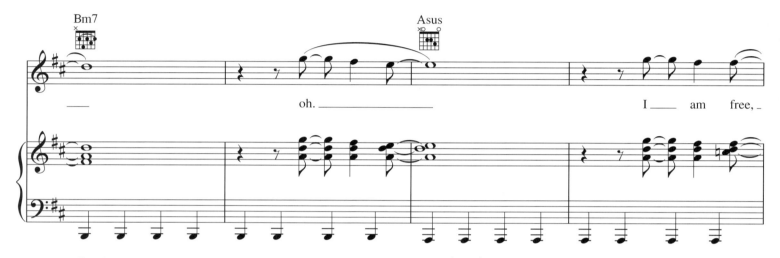

oh. _____ I ___ am free, _

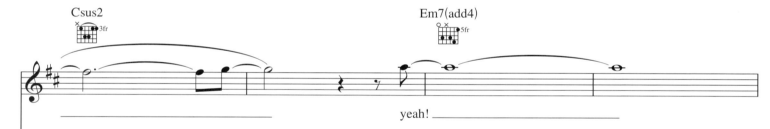

yeah! _____

cresc.

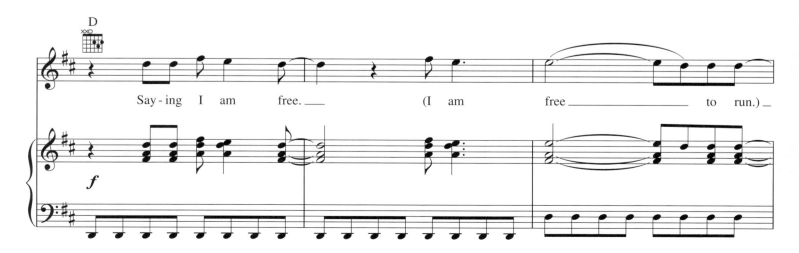

Say-ing I am free. ___ (I am free _____ to run.) _

f

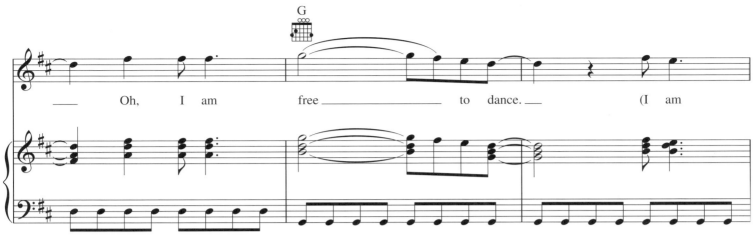

Oh, I am free _____ to dance. ___ (I am

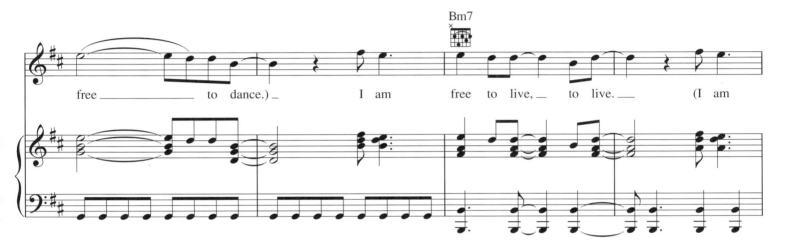

free _____ to dance.) _ I am free to live, ___ to live. ___ (I am

free to live ___ for You.) ___ I am free. ___

Oh, I am free! ___

IN CHRIST ALONE
(with "The Solid Rock")

Words and Music by KEITH GETTY
and STUART TOWNEND

fierc - est drought and storm. What heights of love, what depths of
ones He came to save. 'Til on that cross as Je - sus

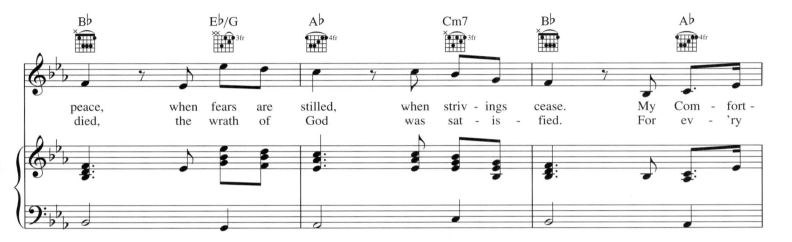

peace, when fears are stilled, when striv - ings cease. My Com - fort -
died, when the wrath of God was sat - is - fied. For ev - 'ry

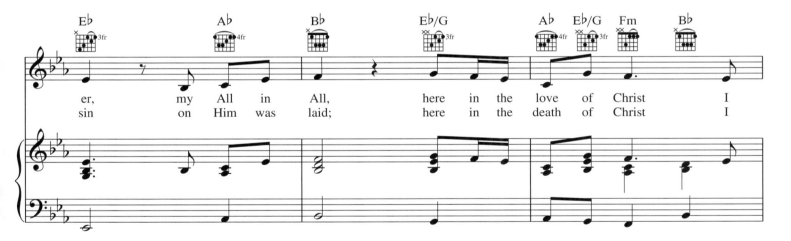

er, my All in All, here in the love of Christ I
sin on Him was laid; here in the death of Christ I

stand. In Christ a - live.

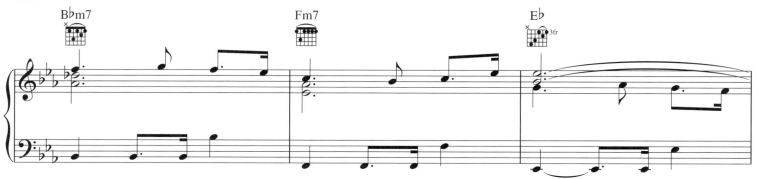

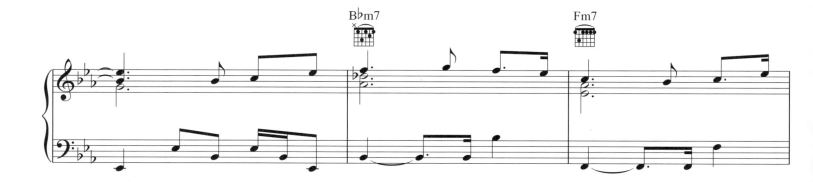

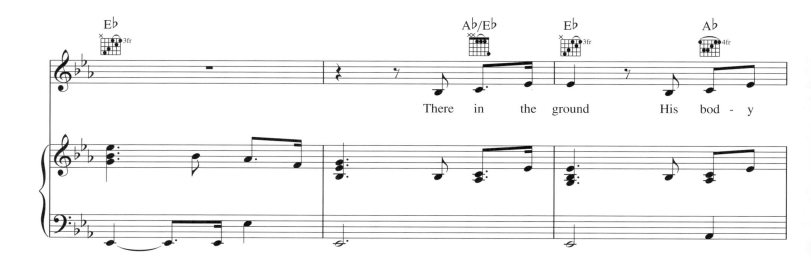

There in the ground His bod - y

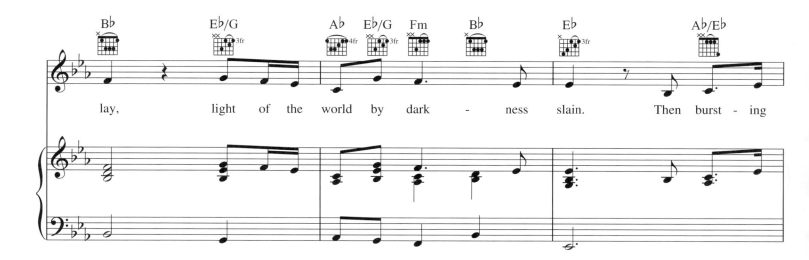

lay, light of the world by dark - ness slain. Then burst - ing

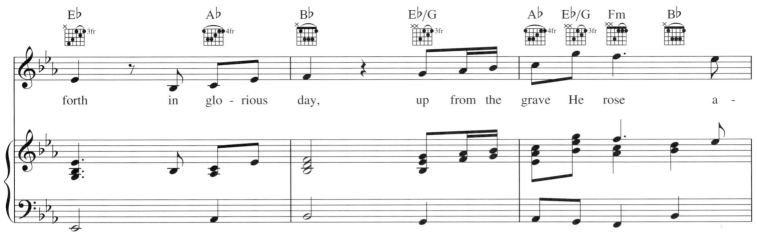

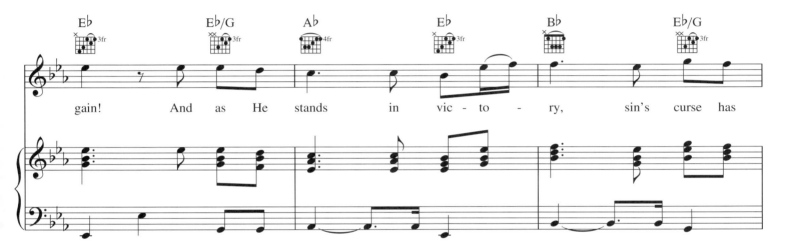

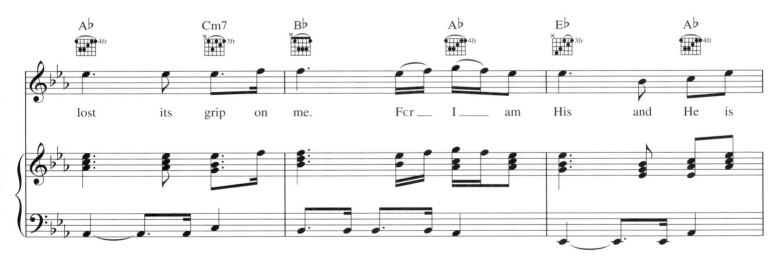

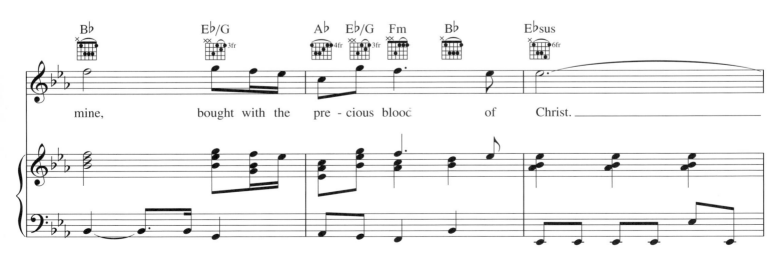

THE SOLID ROCK

Words by EDWARD MOTE
Music by WILLIAM B. BRADBURY
Arranged by TRAVIS COTTRELL
and PAUL MILLS

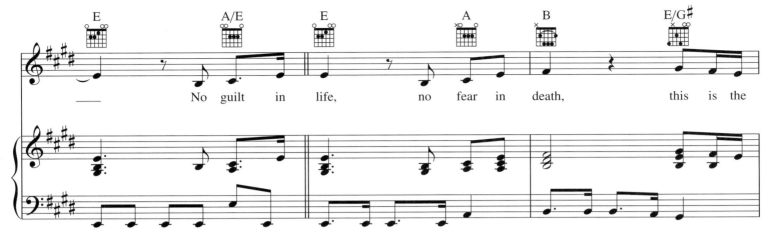

No guilt in life, no fear in death, this is the

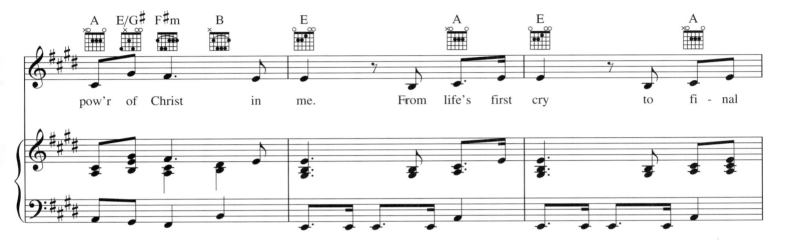

pow'r of Christ in me. From life's first cry to fi - nal

breath, Je - sus com - mands my des - ti - ny. No pow'r of

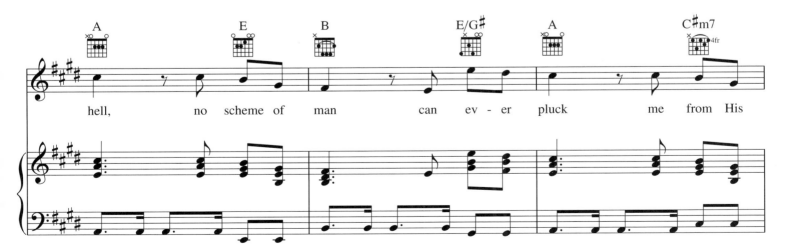

hell, no scheme of man can ev - er pluck me from His

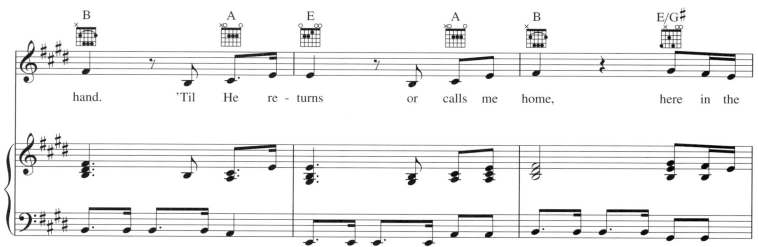

hand. 'Til He re - turns or calls me home, here in the

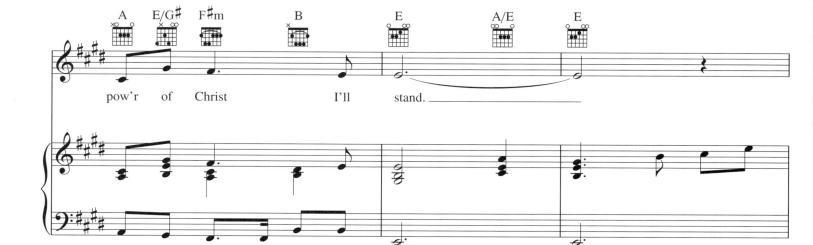

pow'r of Christ I'll stand. _____

LEAD ME TO THE CROSS

Words and Music by
BROOKE FRASER

for my ran - som. _____
now You're ris - en. _____

Ev - 'ry - thing __ I once __ held dear, __ I count __

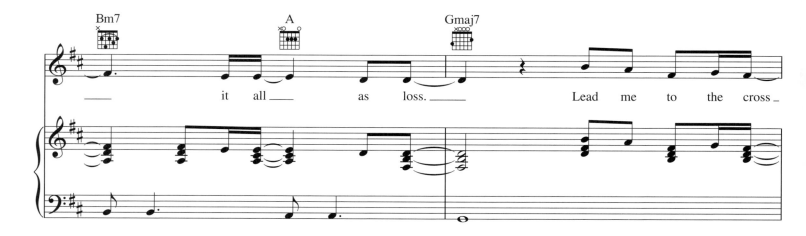

_____ it all __ as loss. _____ Lead me to the cross __

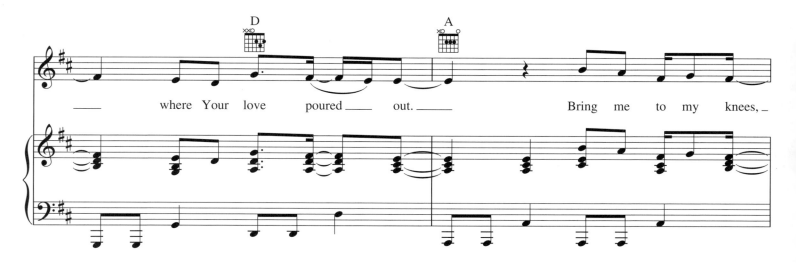

_____ where Your love poured __ out. _____ Bring me to my knees, _

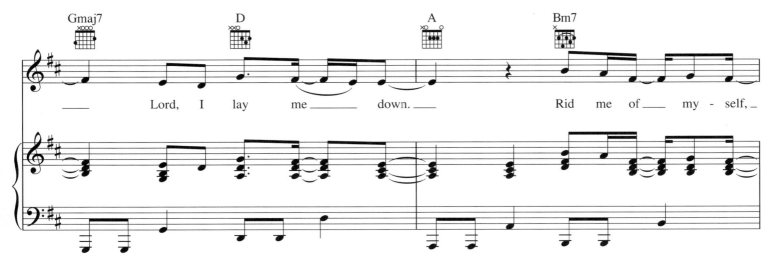

Lord, I lay me _____ down. _____ Rid me of ___ my - self, __

___ I be - long to _____ You. _____ Lead me, _____

lead me to the cross. _____

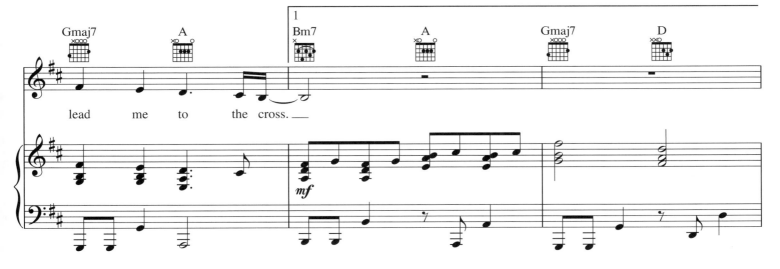

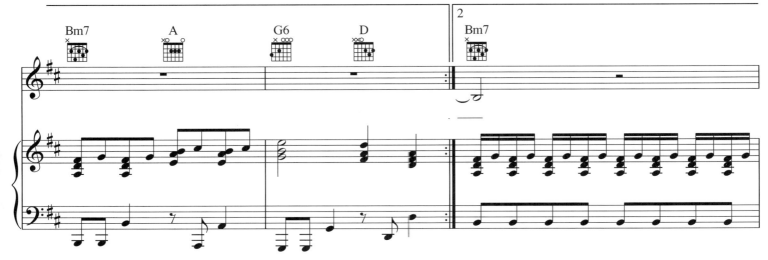

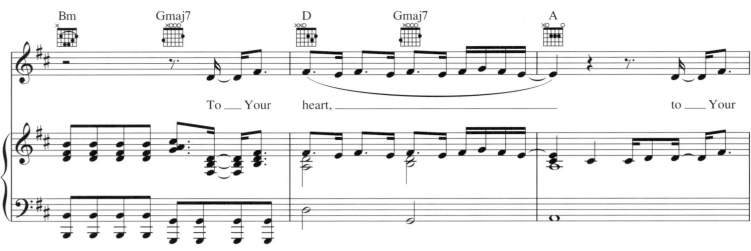

To ___ Your heart, _____ to ___ Your

heart, _____ lead me to ___ Your ___ heart, _____

_____ lead ___ me to ___ Your heart. _____ Lead me to the cross ___

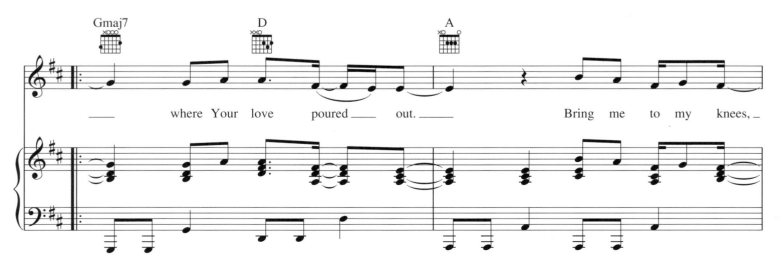

_____ where Your love poured ___ out. ___ Bring me to my knees, ___

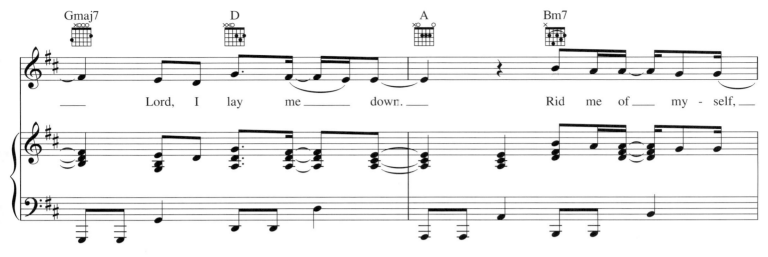

Lord, I lay me down. Rid me of my-self,

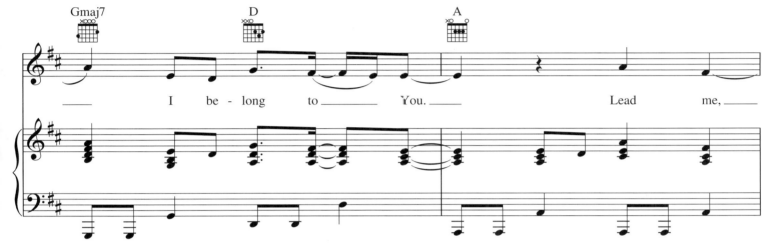

I be-long to You. Lead me,

lead me. Lead me to the cross

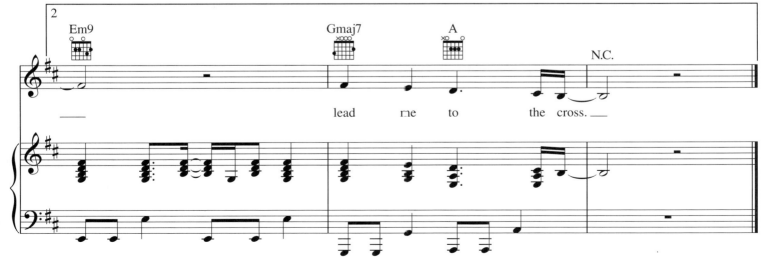

lead me to the cross.

LOVE THE LORD

Words and Music by
LINCOLN BREWSTER

Da da dum da da dum da da da. ___ Da da dum da da dum da da da. ___

___ Da da dum oh, ___ yeah. ___

Love the Lord ___ your God ___ with all ___ your heart, ___ with all ___ your soul, ___ with all ___ your mind ___
I will serve ___ the Lord ___ with all ___ my heart, ___ with all ___ my soul, ___ with all ___ my mind ___

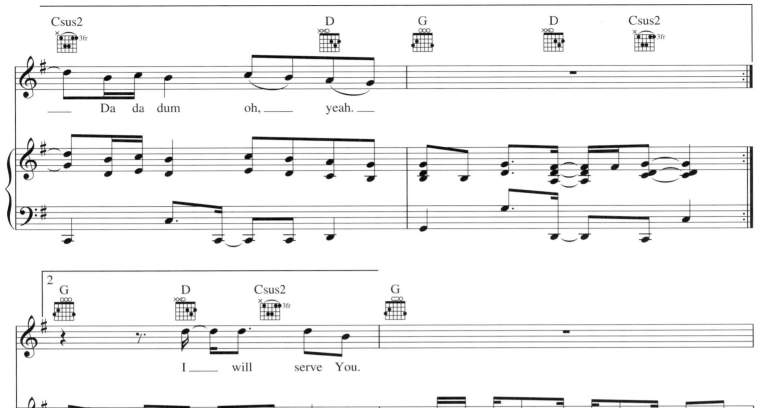

Da da dum oh, ____ yeah. ____

I ____ will serve You.

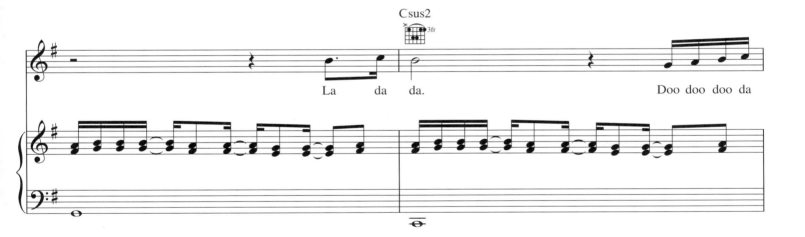

La da da.

Doo doo doo da

da dee da ____ da da ____ da da ____ da da. ____

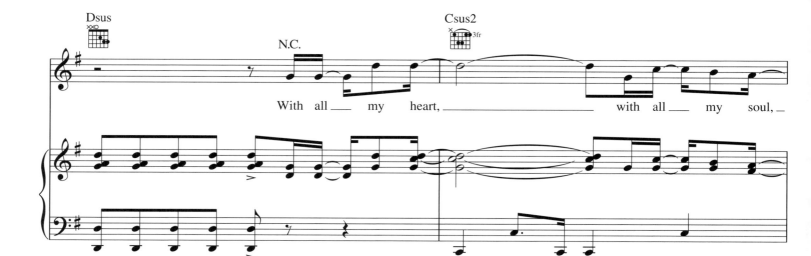

With all ___ my heart, _____ with all ___ my soul, _

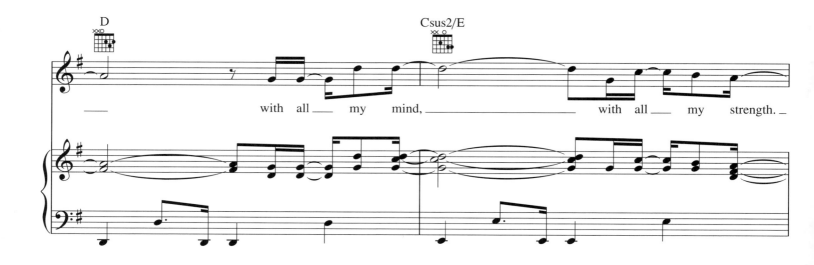

___ with all ___ my mind, _____ with all ___ my strength. _

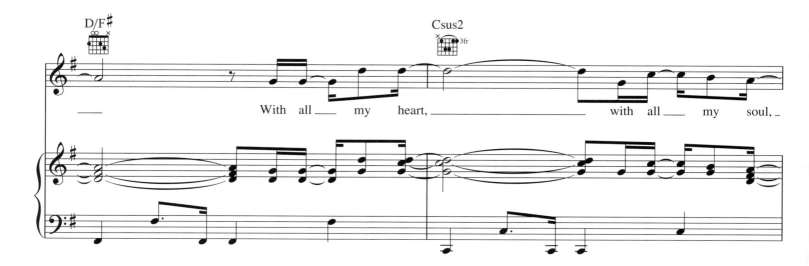

___ With all ___ my heart, _____ with all ___ my soul, _

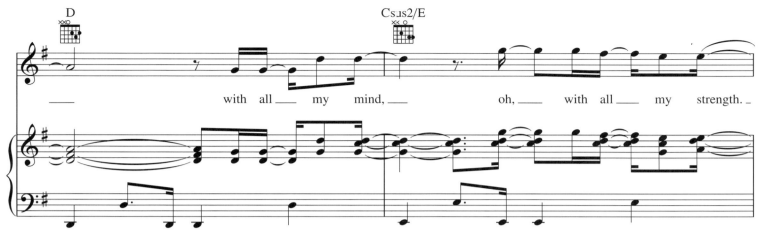

with all ___ my mind, ___ oh, ___ with all ___ my strength. ___

_____ I will love ___ You, Lord, ___ with all ___ my heart, ___

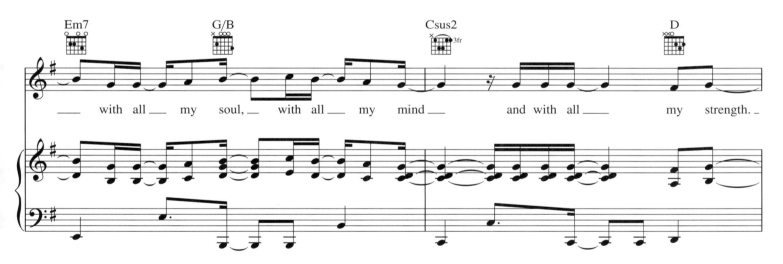

___ with all ___ my soul, ___ with all ___ my mind ___ and with all ___ my strength. ___

___ I will love ___ You, Lord, ___ with all ___ my heart, ___

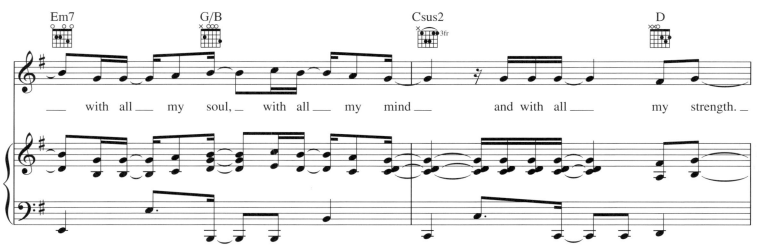

with all __ my soul, __ with all __ my mind __ and with all ___ my strength. __

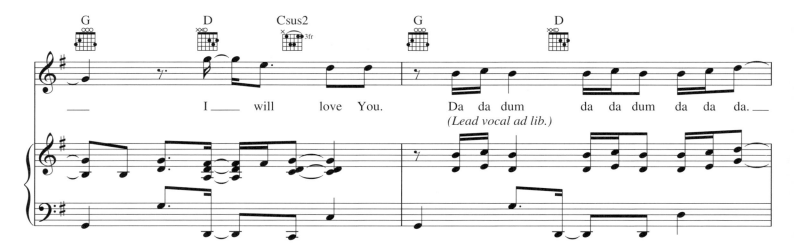

__ I ___ will love You. Da da dum da da dum da da da. __
(Lead vocal ad lib.)

__ Da da dum da da dum da da da. __ Da da dum oh, ___ yeah. __

Da da dum da da dum da da da. __

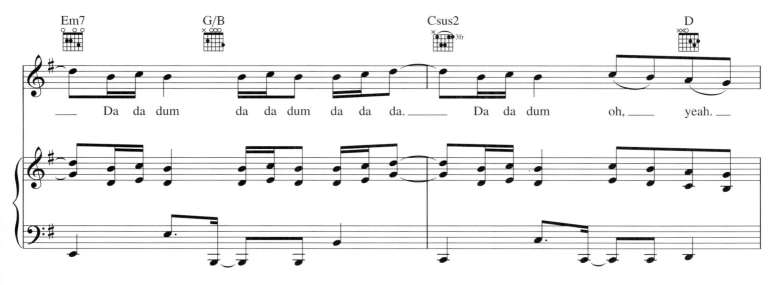

Da da dum da da dum da da da.___ Da da dum oh,___ yeah.___

I will love __ You, Lord, __ with all __ my heart, __

___ with all __ my soul, __ with all __ my mind __ and with all __ my strength. __

rit.

MIGHTY TO SAVE

Words and Music by BEN FIELDING
and REUBEN MORGAN

Moderately, in 2

Well,
So

ev - 'ry - one needs com - pas - sion, a love that's nev - er fail -
take ___ me as You find ___ me, all my fears and fail -

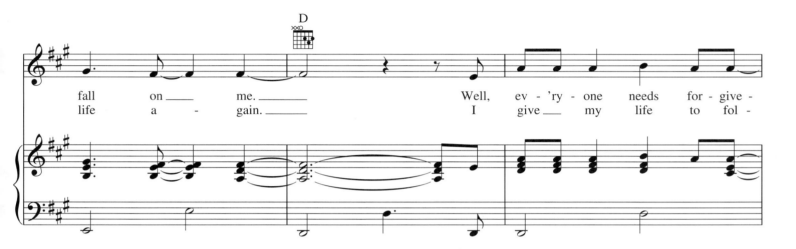

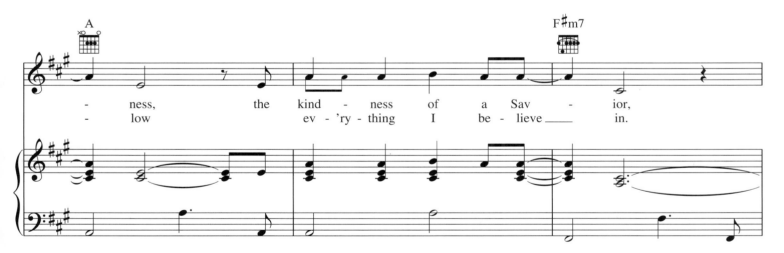

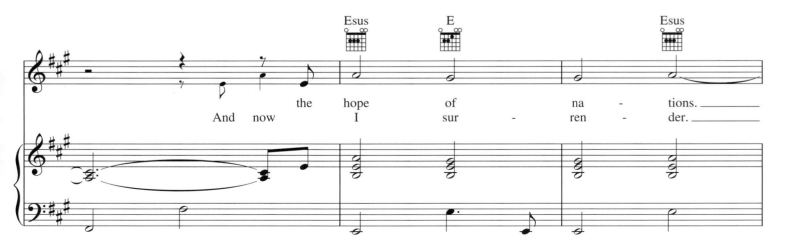

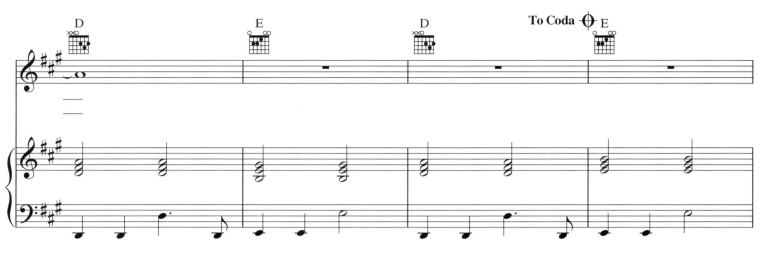

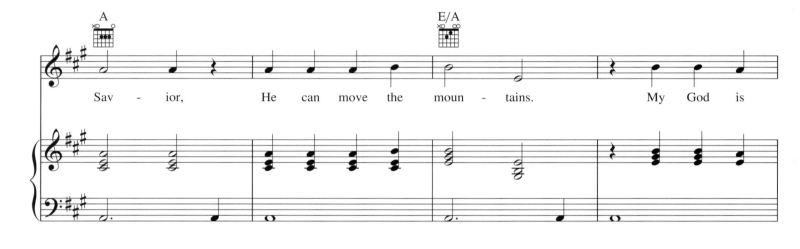

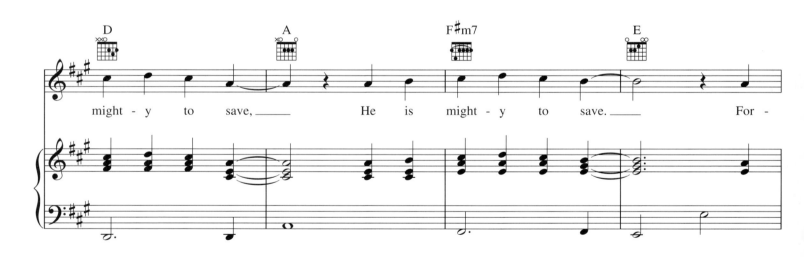

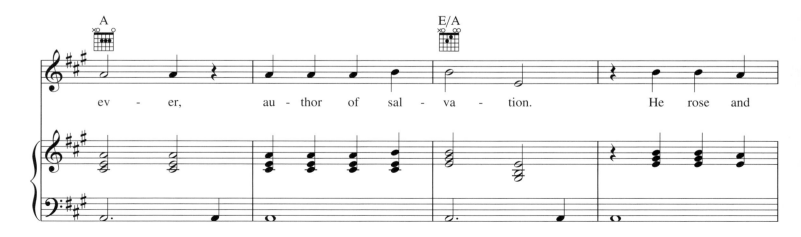

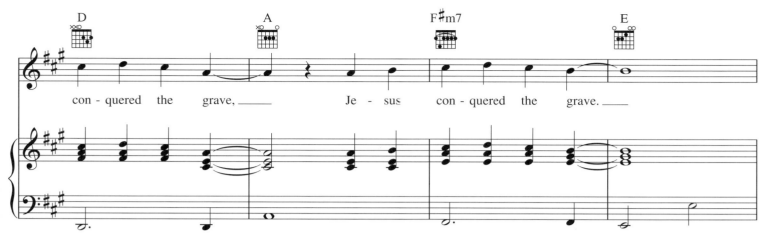

con - quered the grave, _____ Je - sus con - quered the grave. _____

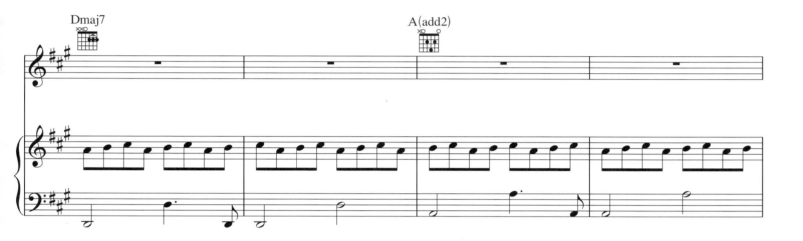

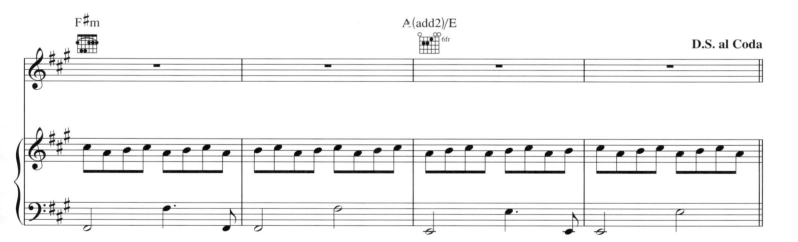

D.S. al Coda

Sav - ior, He can move the

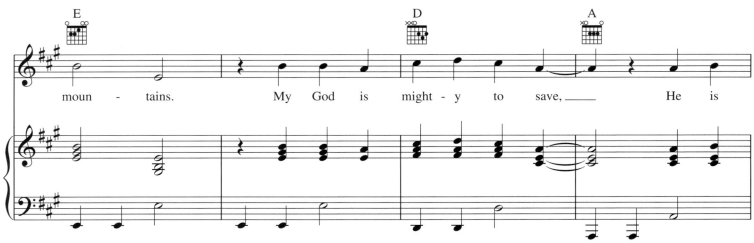

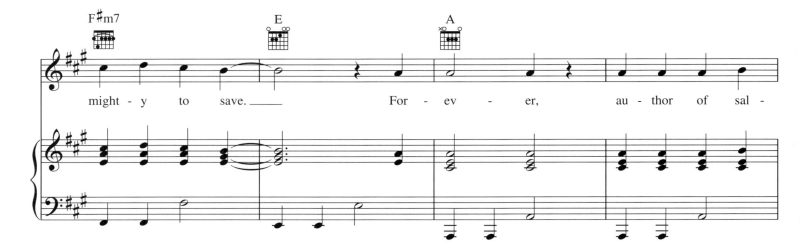

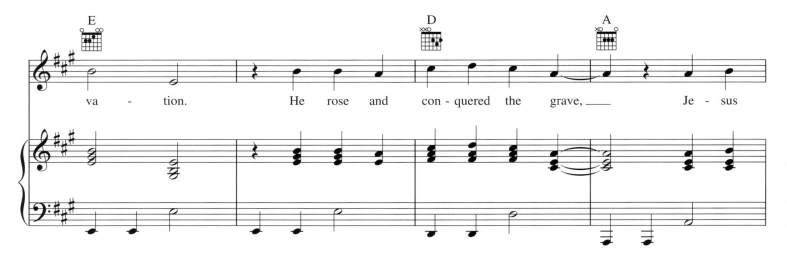

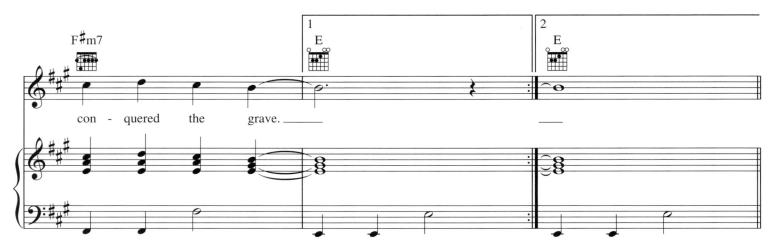

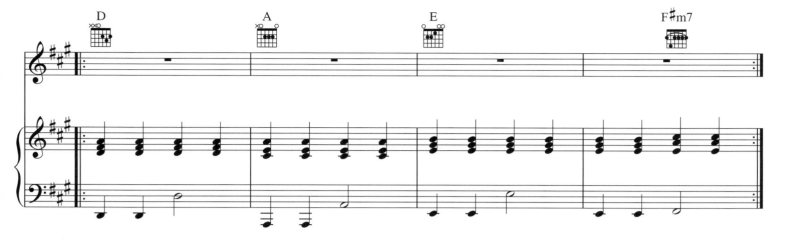

Shine Your light and let the whole world ___ see. Sing- in'

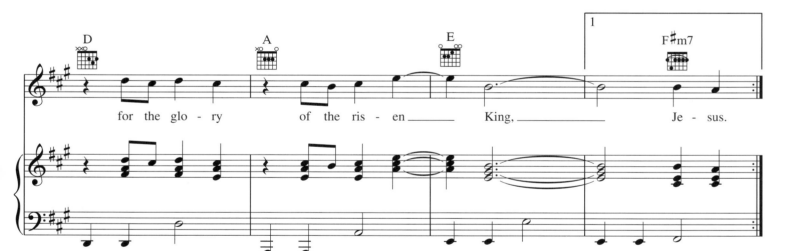

for the glo - ry of the ris - en ___ King, ___ Je - sus.

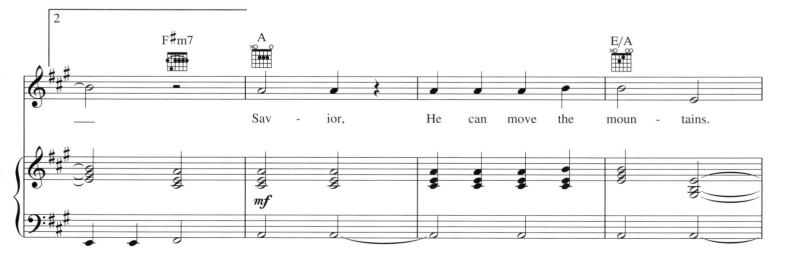

___ Sav - ior, He can move the moun - tains.

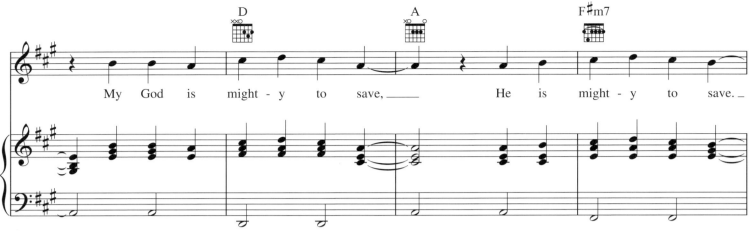

My God is might-y to save, _____ He is might-y to save. _

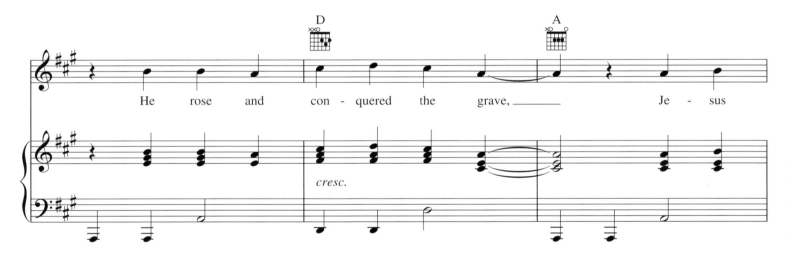

_ For - ev - er, au - thor of sal - va - tion.

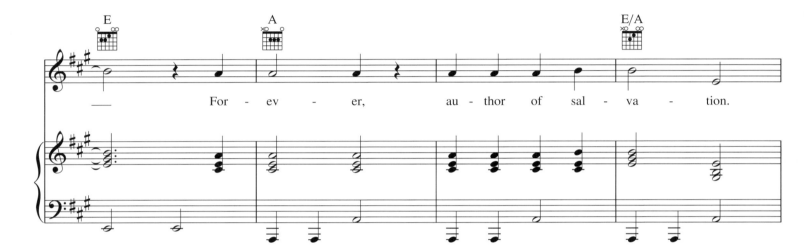

He rose and con - quered the grave, _____ Je - sus

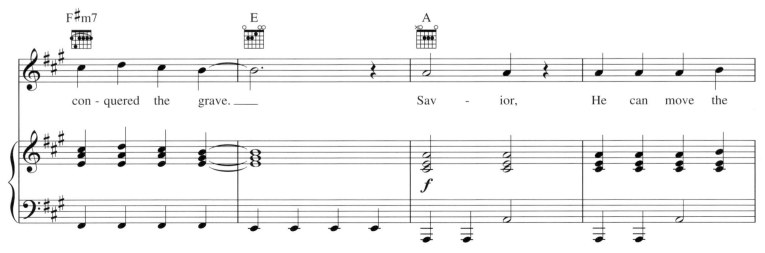

con - quered the grave. ____ Sav - ior, He can move the

moun - tains. My God is might - y to save, ___

___ He is might - y to save. ___ For -

ev - er, au - thor of sal - va - tion.

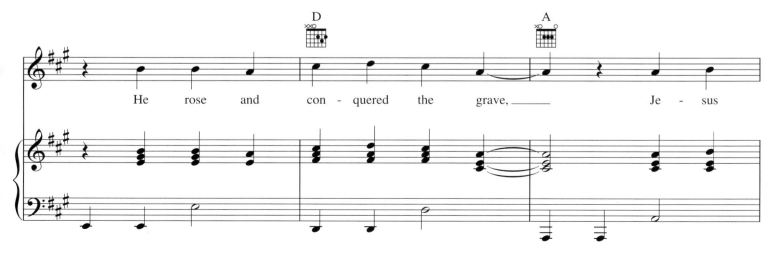

He rose and con - quered the grave, ___ Je - sus

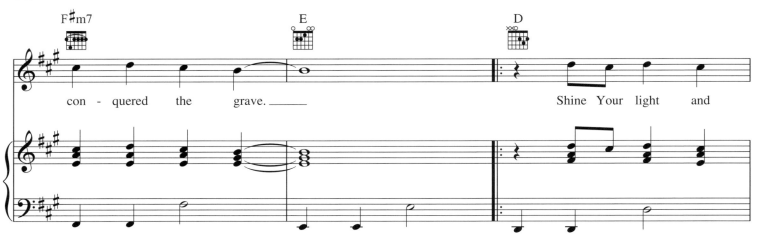

con - quered the grave. _____ Shine Your light and

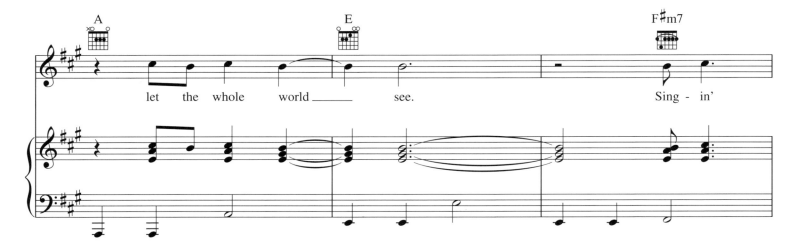

let the whole world _____ see. Sing - in'

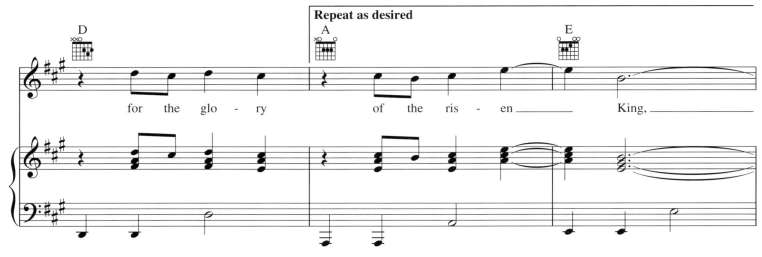

Repeat as desired

for the glo - ry of the ris - en _____ King, _____

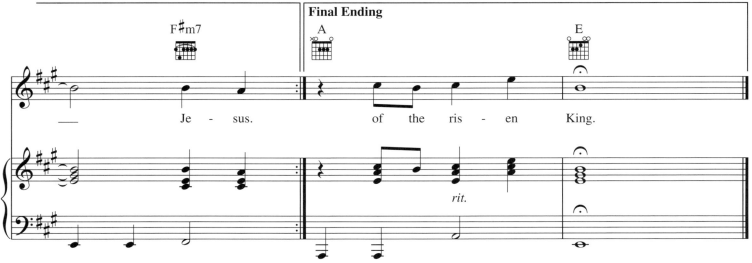

Final Ending

_____ Je - sus. of the ris - en King.

rit.

YOUR NAME

Words and Music by PAUL BALOCHE
and GLENN PACKIAM

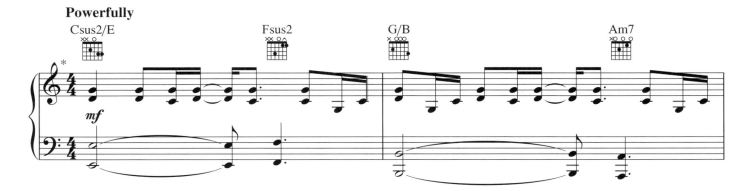

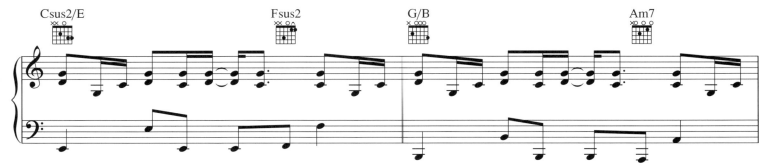

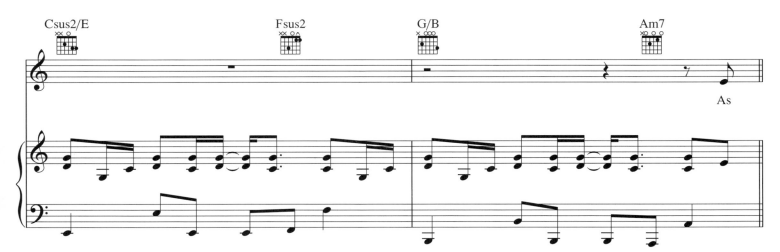

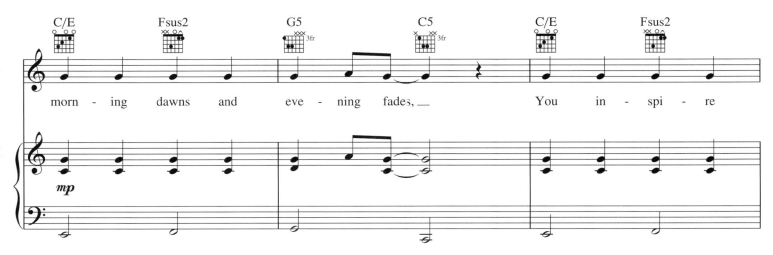

* *Recorded a half step lower.*

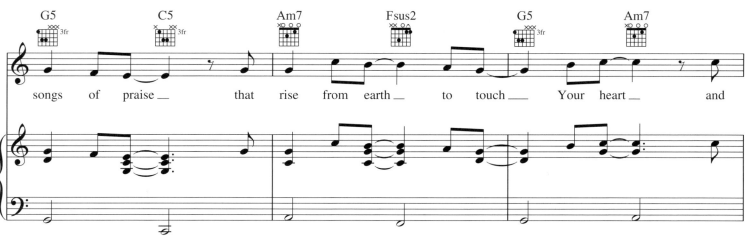

songs of praise __ that rise from earth __ to touch __ Your heart __ and

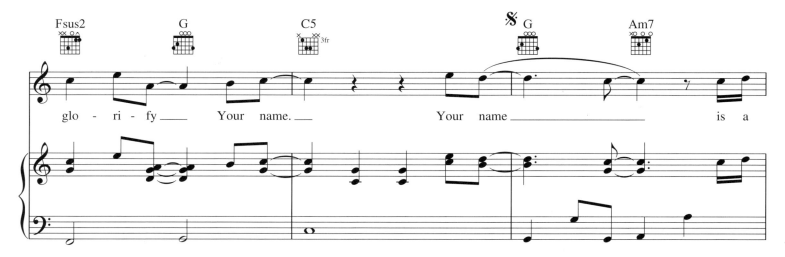

glo - ri - fy __ Your name. __ Your name _____ is a

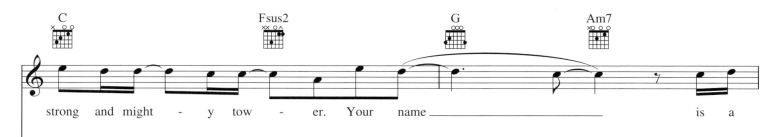

strong and might - y tow - er. Your name _____ is a

shel - ter like __ no oth - er. Your name, _____ let the

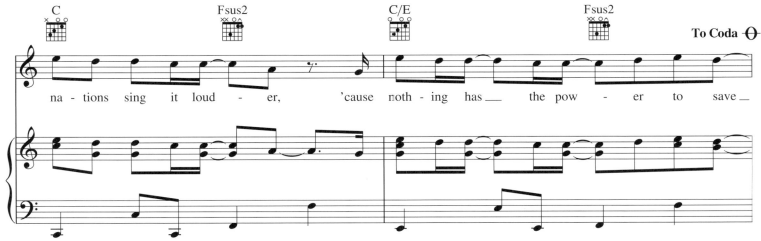

na - tions sing it loud - er, 'cause noth - ing has ___ the pow - er to save ___

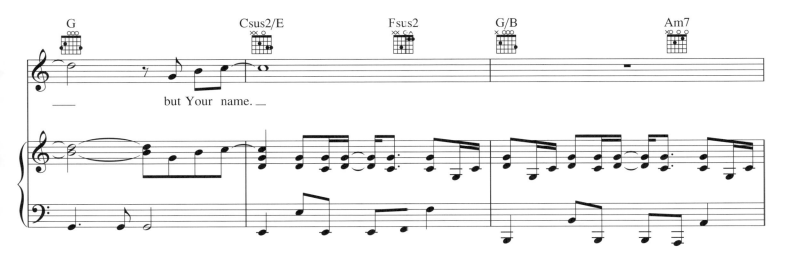

___ but Your name. ___

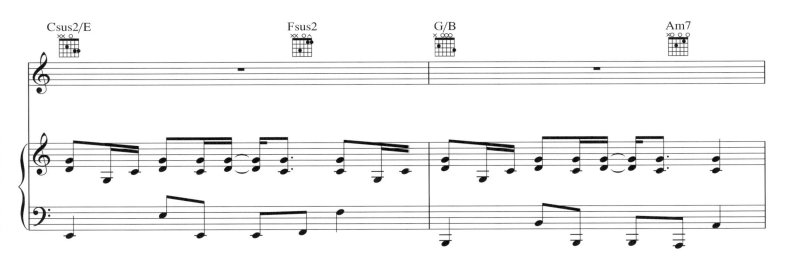

Je - sus, in Your name we pray, ___ come and fill our ___

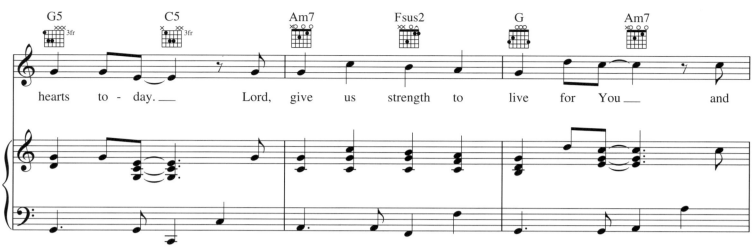

hearts to - day. ___ Lord, give us strength to live for You ___ and

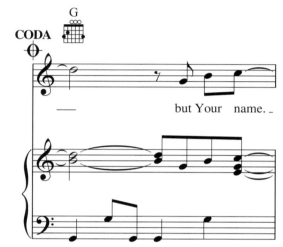

glo - ri - fy ___ Your name. _____ Your name _   but Your name. _

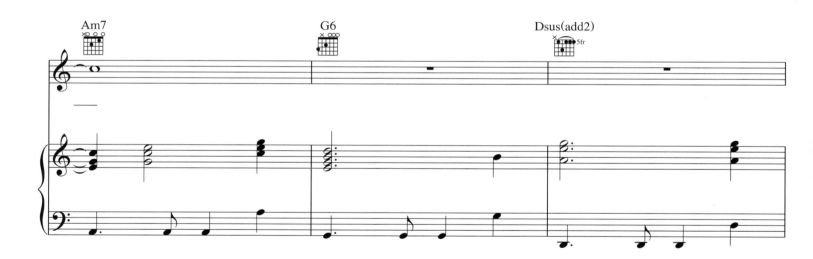

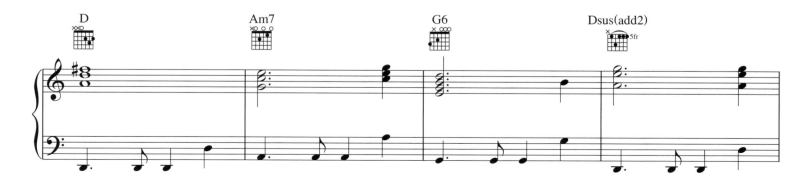

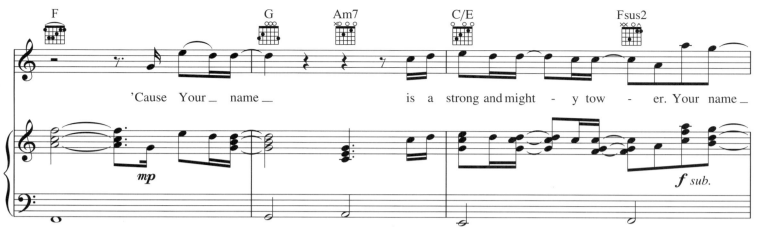

'Cause Your __ name __ is a strong and mighty tow - er. Your name __

__ is a shel - ter like __ no oth - er. Your name, __

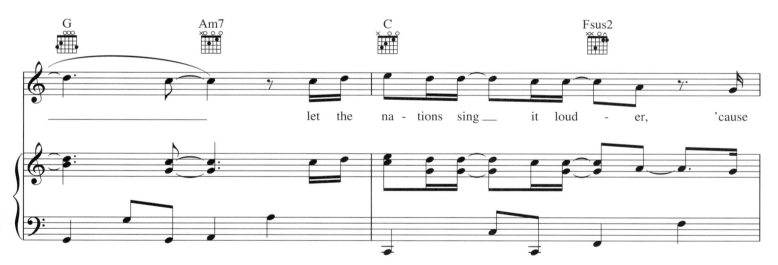

let the na - tions sing __ it loud - er, 'cause

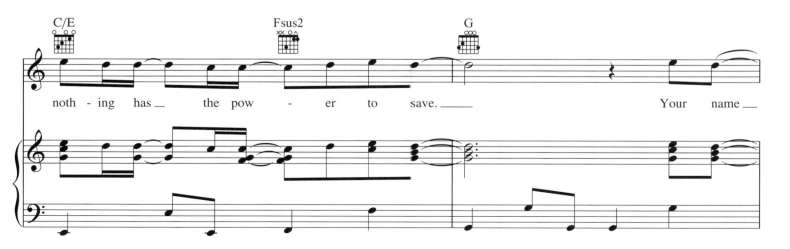

noth - ing has __ the pow - er to save. ___ Your name __

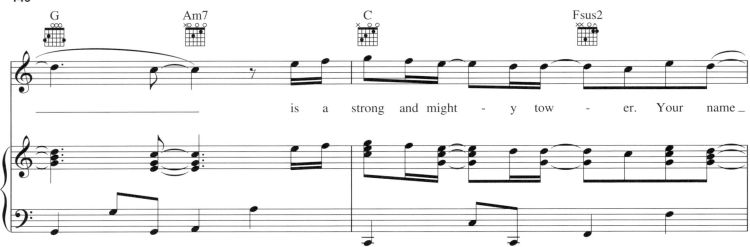

is a strong and might - y tow - er. Your name ___

is a shel - ter like ___ no oth - er. Your name, ___

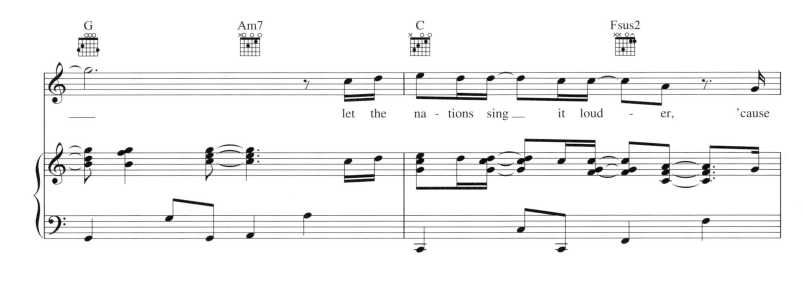

___ let the na - tions sing ___ it loud - er, 'cause

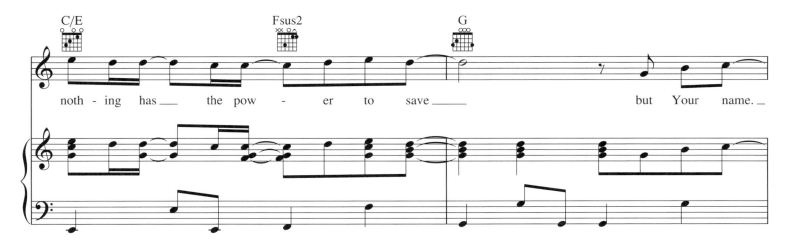

noth - ing has ___ the pow - er to save ___ but Your name. ___

Na na na na na na. Na na na na na na.

Na na na na na na. Na na na na na na.

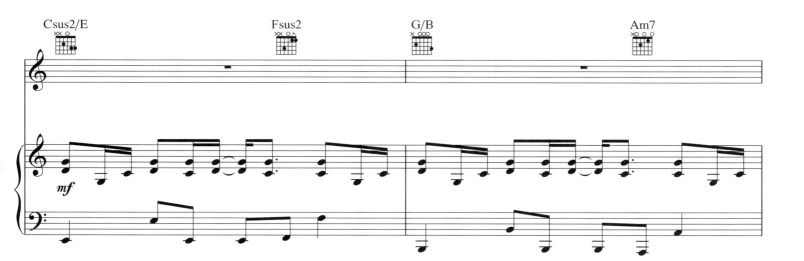

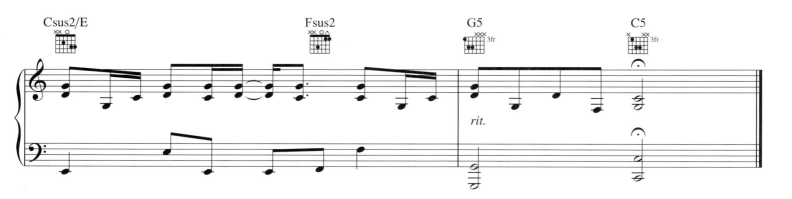

rit.

MOVING FORWARD

Words and Music by ISRAEL HOUGHTON
and RICARDO SANCHEZ

With movement

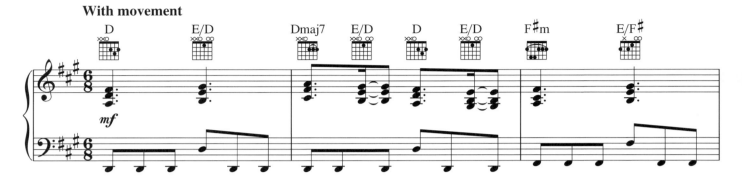

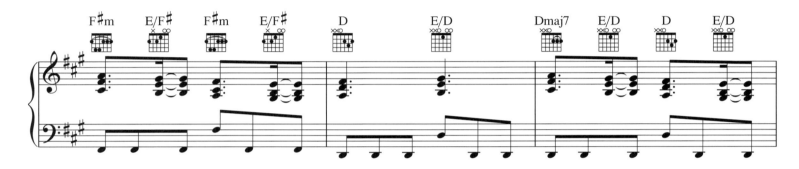

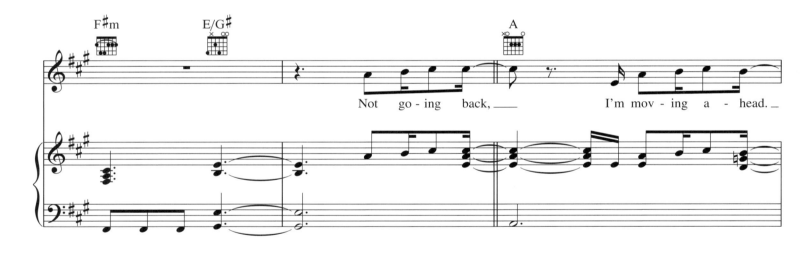

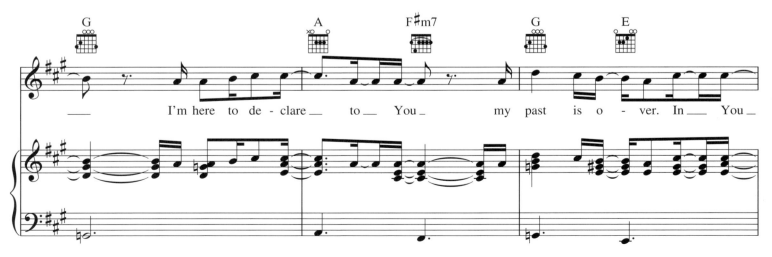

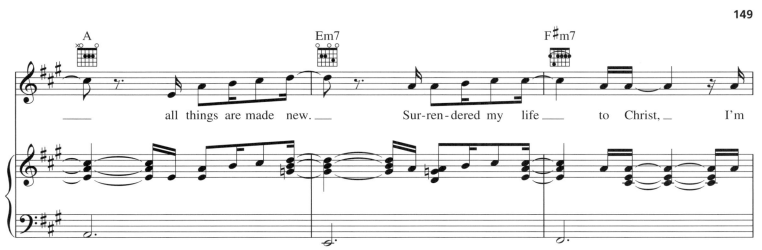

all things are made new. ___ Sur-ren-dered my life ___ to Christ, ___ I'm

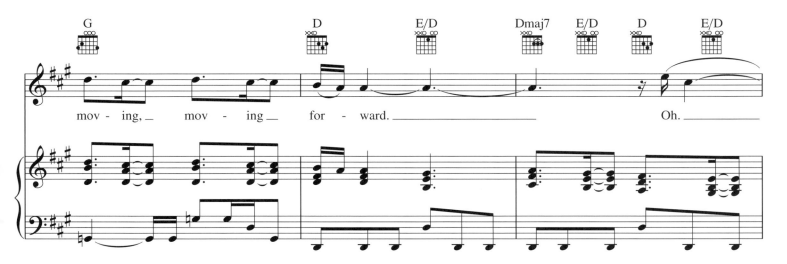

mov-ing, ___ mov-ing ___ for - ward. _____ Oh. _____

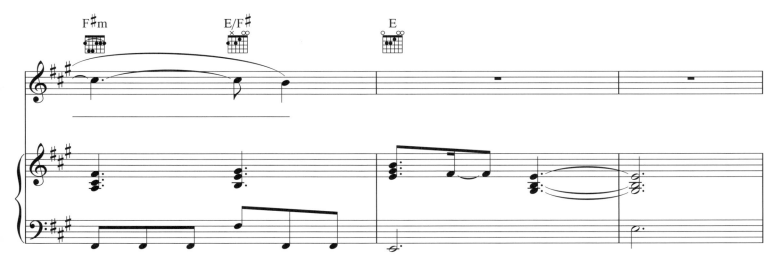

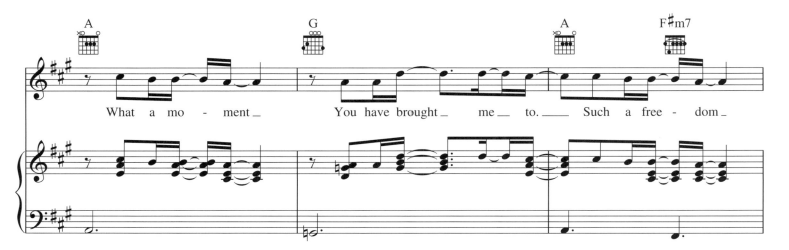

What a mo - ment ___ You have brought ___ me to. ___ Such a free - dom ___

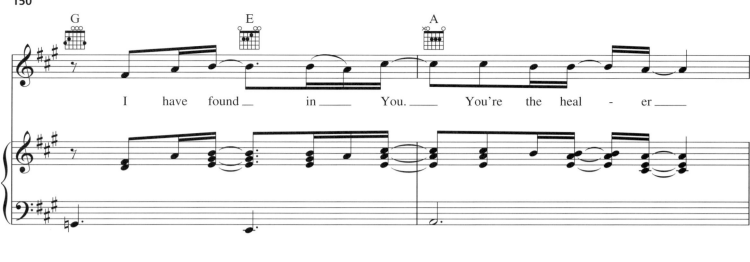

I have found ___ in ___ You. ___ You're the heal - er ___

who makes all things ___ new, ___ yeah, ___ yeah, ___ yeah. ___

___ Not go - ing back, ___ I'm mov - ing a - head.

___ I'm here to de - clare ___ to ___ You ___ my

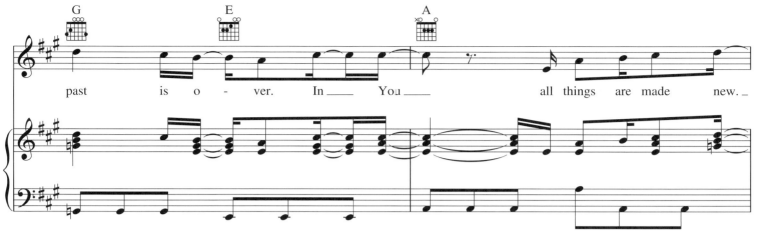

past is o - ver. In ____ You ____ all things are made new. ____

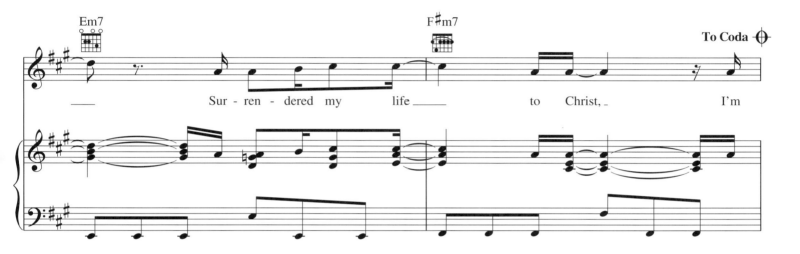

To Coda ✛

____ Sur - ren - dered my life ____ to Christ, ____ I'm

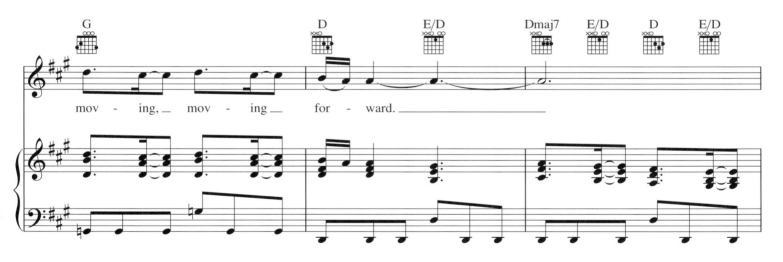

mov - ing, ____ mov - ing ____ for - ward. _____

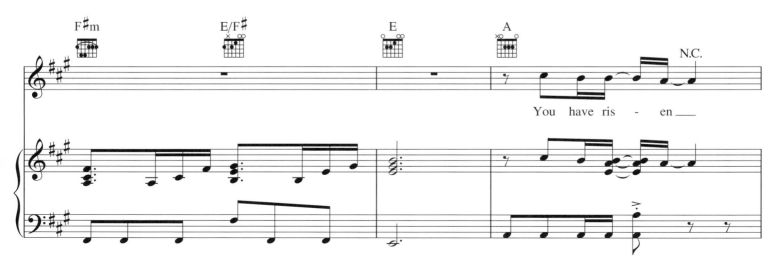

You have ris - en ____

with all pow-er in Your hands.___ You have giv-en me

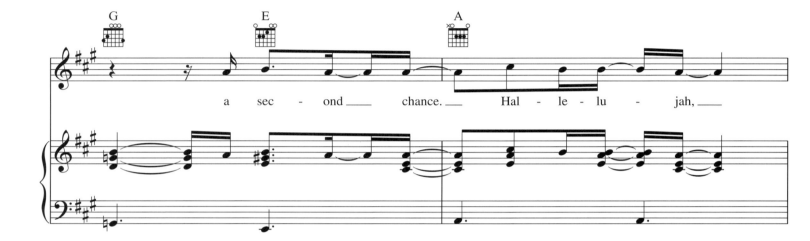

a sec-ond___ chance.___ Hal-le-lu-___jah,___

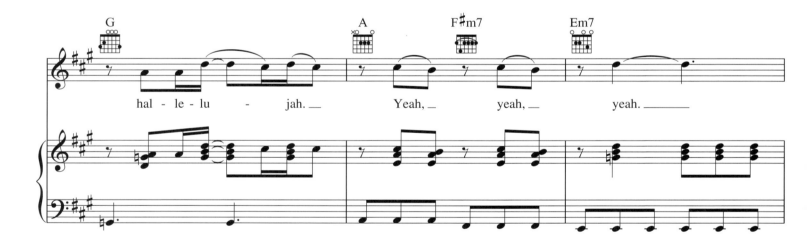

hal-le-lu-___jah.___ Yeah,___ yeah,___ yeah._____

D.S. al Coda

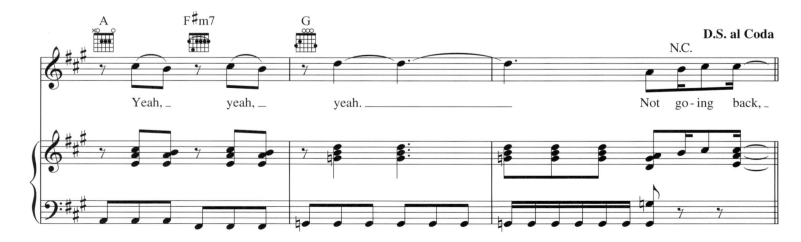

Yeah,___ yeah,___ yeah._____ Not go-ing back,___

CODA

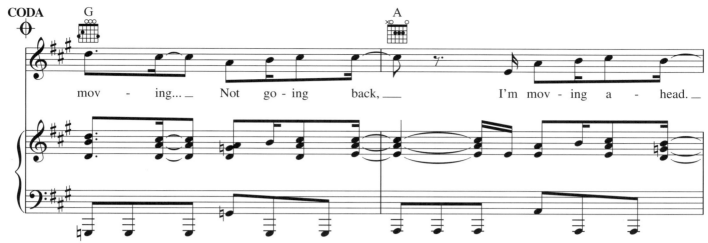

mov - ing... __ Not go - ing back, ___ I'm mov - ing a - head. __

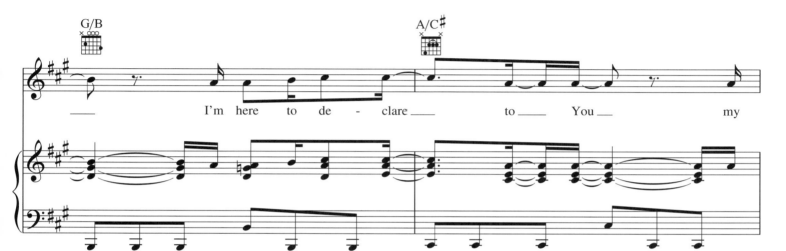

___ I'm here to de - clare ___ to ___ You ___ my

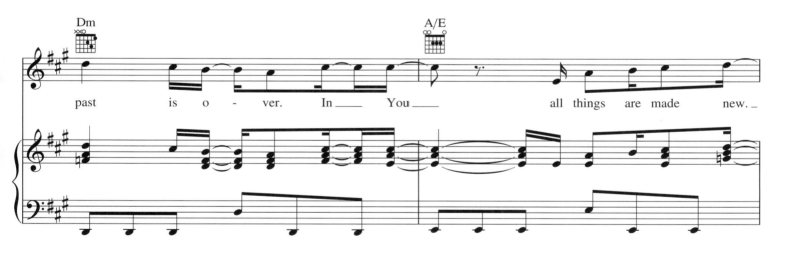

past is o - ver. In ___ You ___ all things are made new. __

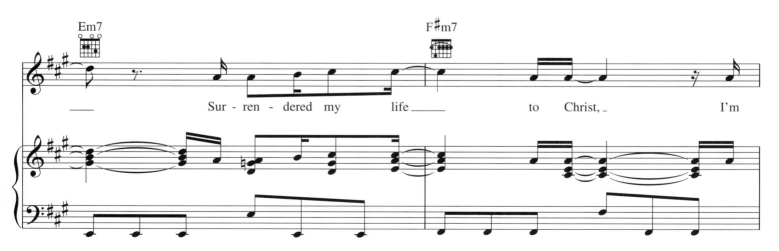

___ Sur - ren - dered my life ___ to Christ, __ I'm

OPEN THE EYES OF MY HEART

Words and Music by
PAUL BALOCHE

Medium bright Pop

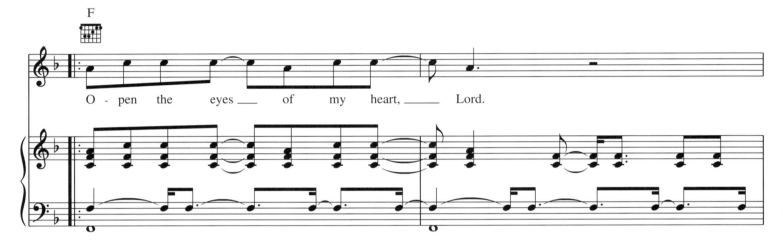

O - pen the eyes ___ of my heart, ___ Lord.

O - pen the eyes ___ of my heart. ___ I want ___ to

see ___ You. ___ I want ___ to see ___ You. ___

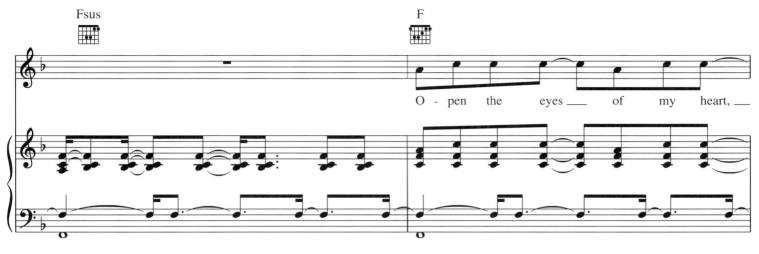

Fsus   F

O - pen the eyes ___ of my heart, ___

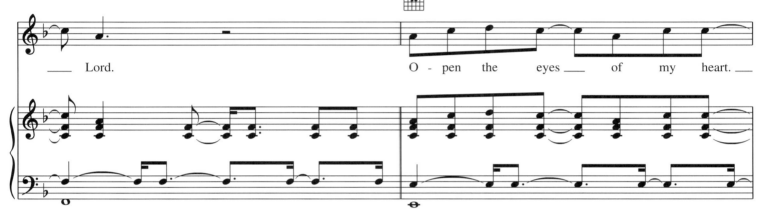

F/E

___ Lord.   O - pen the eyes ___ of my heart. ___

B♭sus2

___ I want _ to see ____ You. ___

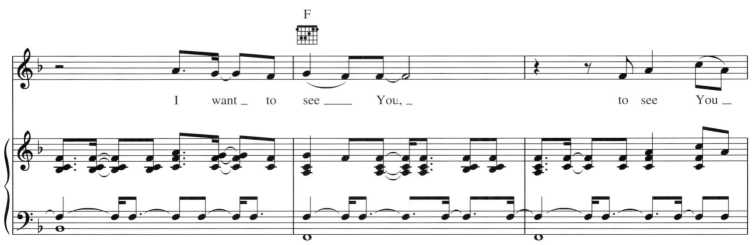

F

I want _ to see ___ You, _   to see You _

high and lift - ed up, shin -

- ing in the light of Your glo - ry.

Pour out __ Your pow - er and love ___ as we sing ho - ly, ho - ly, ho -

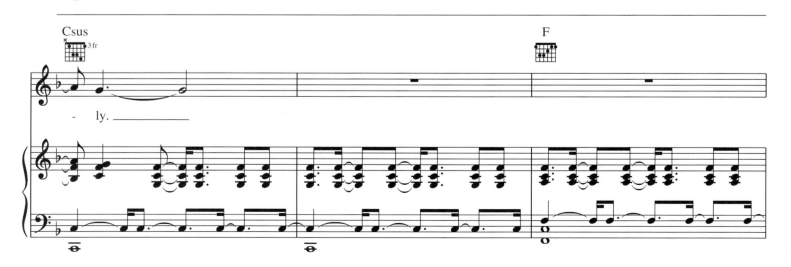

- ly. _____

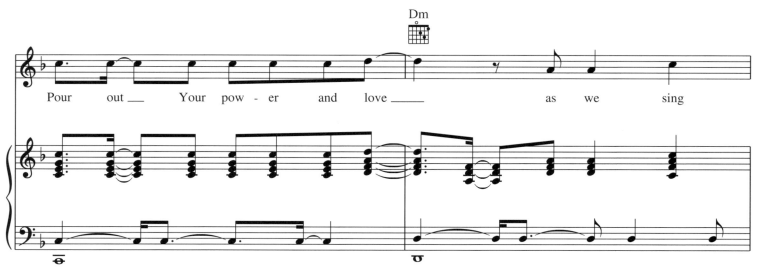

Pour out __ Your pow -er and love _____ as we sing

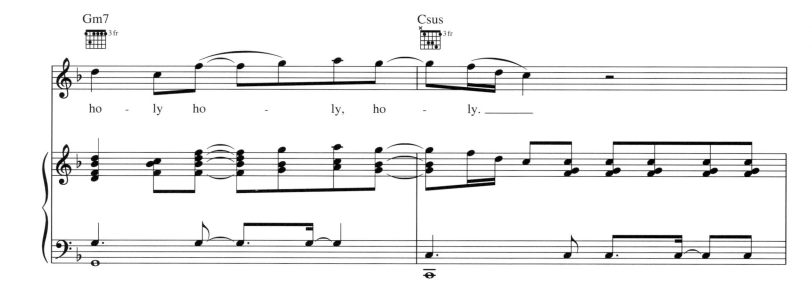

ho - ly ho - ly, ho - ly. _____

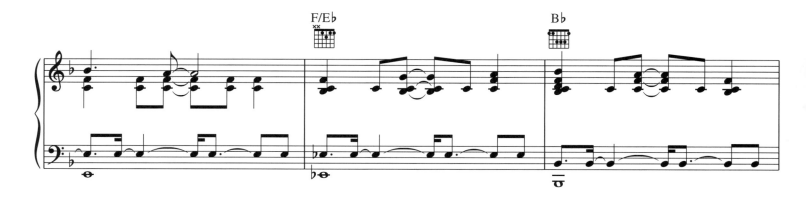

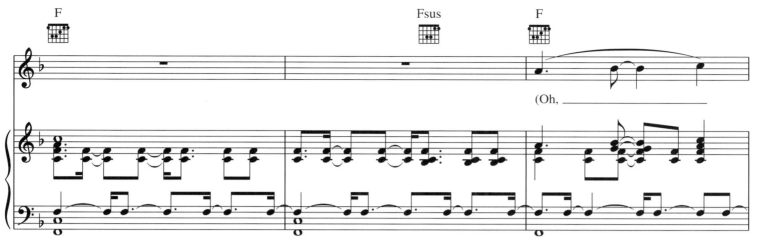

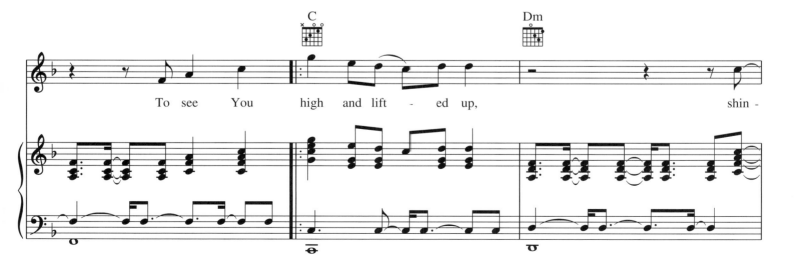

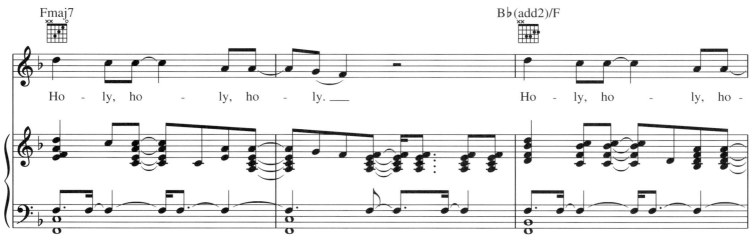

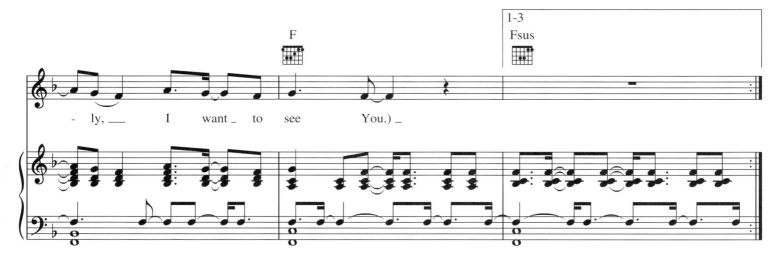

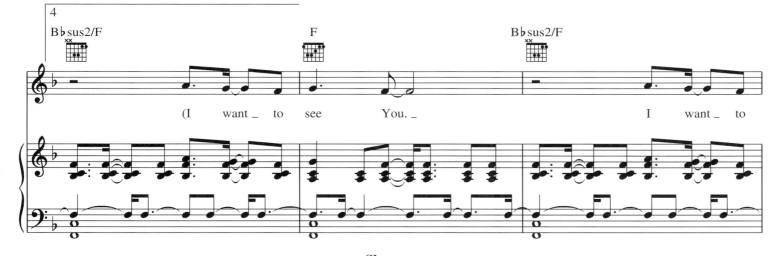

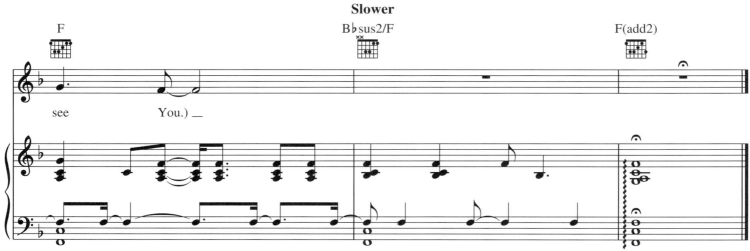

REVELATION SONG

Words and Music by
JENNIE LEE RIDDLE

Wor - thy is the

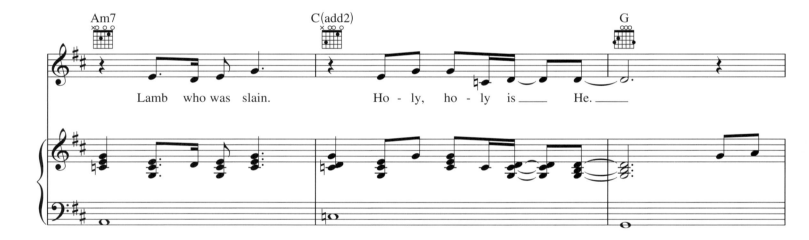

Lamb who was slain. Ho - ly, ho - ly is ___ He. ___

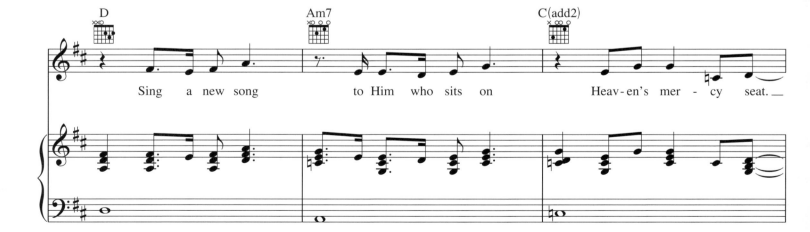

Sing a new song to Him who sits on Heav-en's mer - cy seat. ___

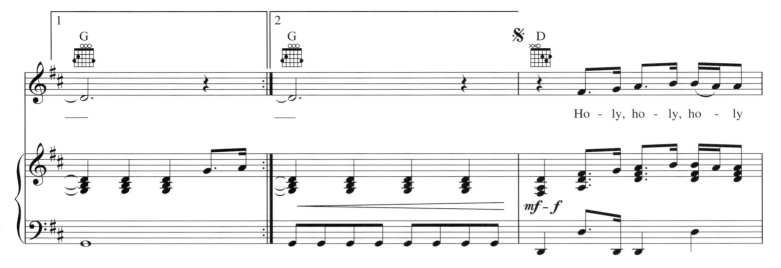

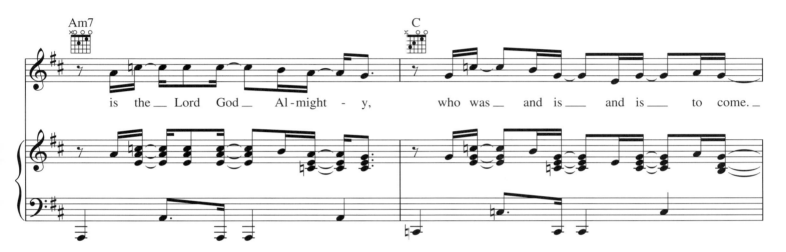

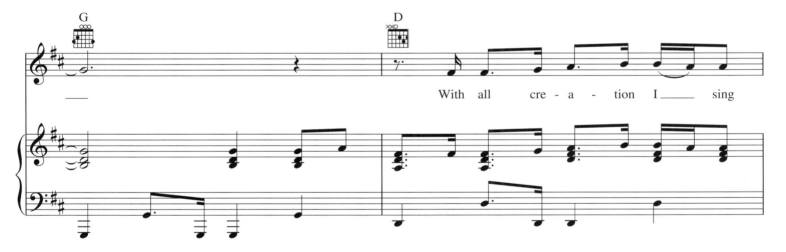

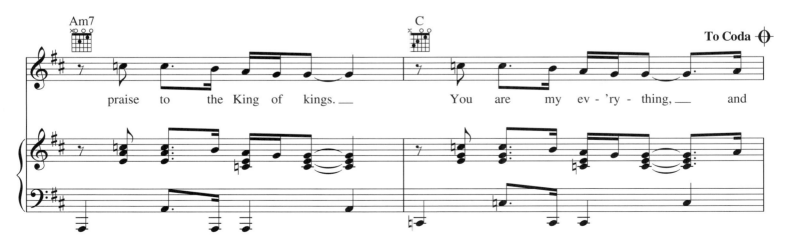

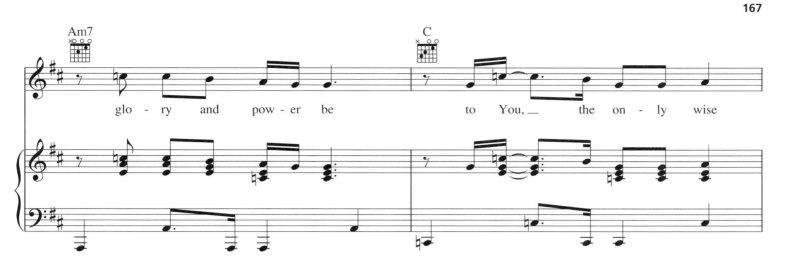

glory and pow-er be to You, __ the on-ly wise

King, oh. _____

CODA

I will __ a-dore You. _____

__ I _____ will. I ____ a-dore __

_____ You. _____ Filled with won-der,

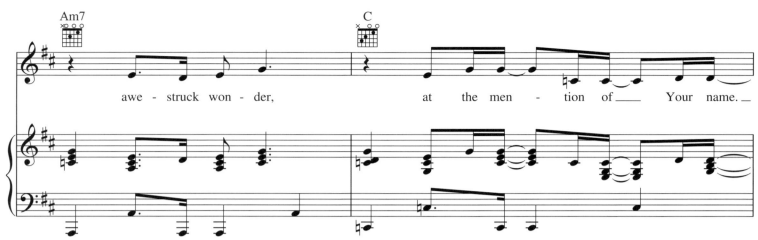

awe - struck won - der, at the men - tion of ___ Your name. __

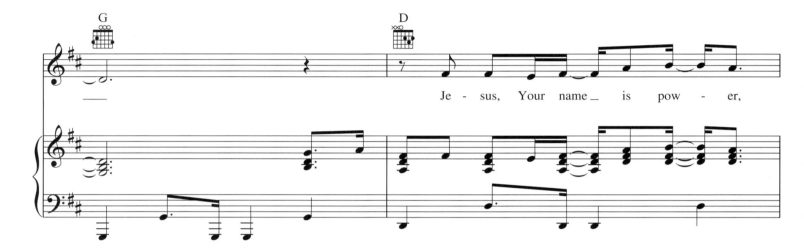

__ Je - sus, Your name __ is pow - er,

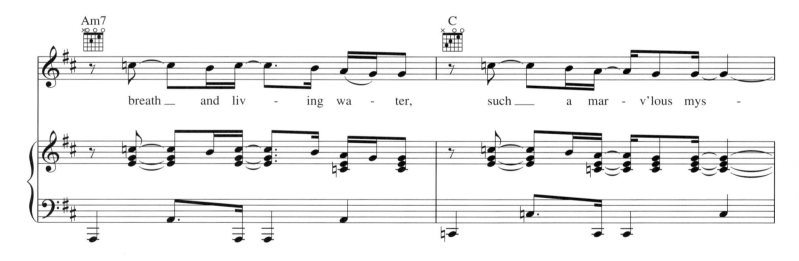

breath __ and liv - ing wa - ter, such __ a mar - v'lous mys -

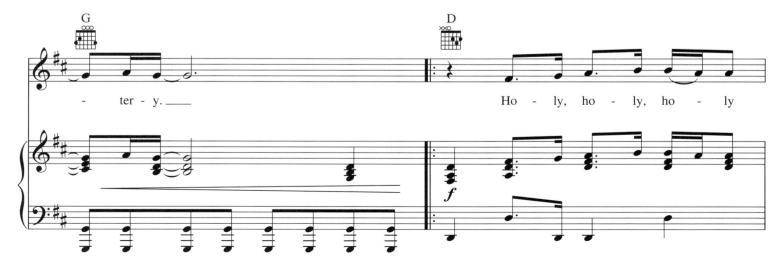

- ter - y. ___ Ho - ly, ho - ly, ho - ly

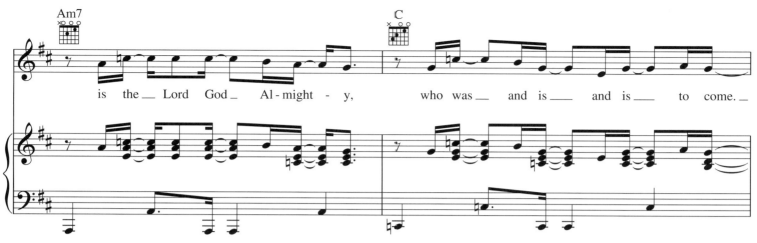

is the __ Lord God __ Al-might - y, who was __ and is __ and is __ to come. __

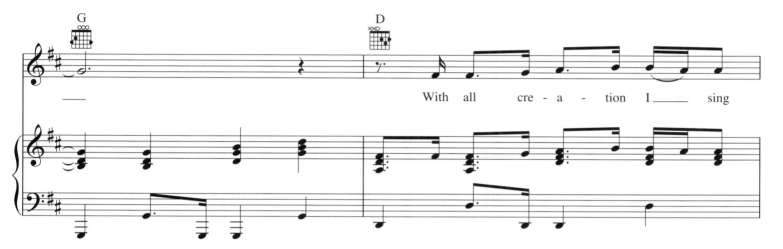

__ With all cre - a - tion I _____ sing

praise to the King of kings. __ You are my ev-'ry-thing, __ and

I will __ a-dore You. I will __ a-dore You. __

TODAY IS THE DAY

Words and Music by LINCOLN BREWSTER
and PAUL BALOCHE

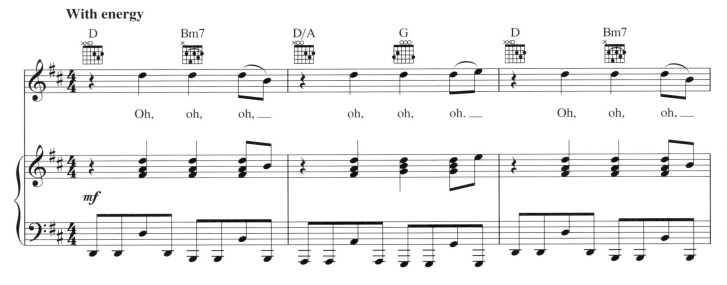

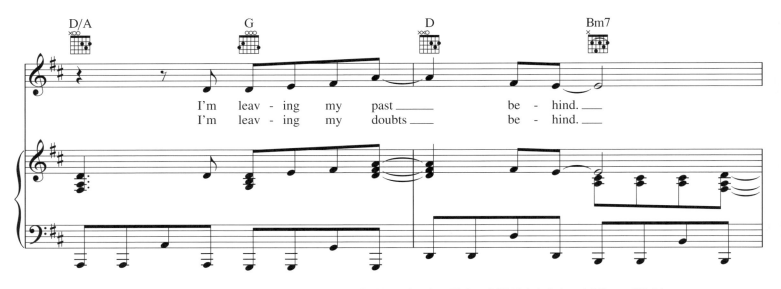

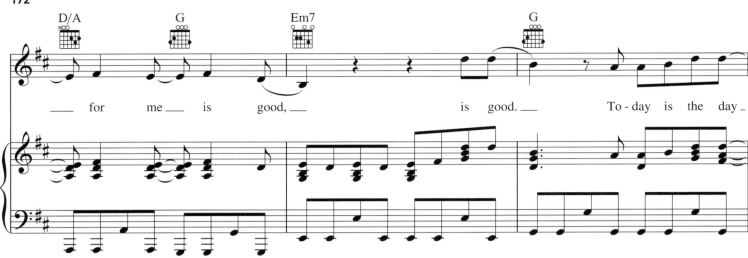

for me __ is good, __ is good. __ To - day is the day __

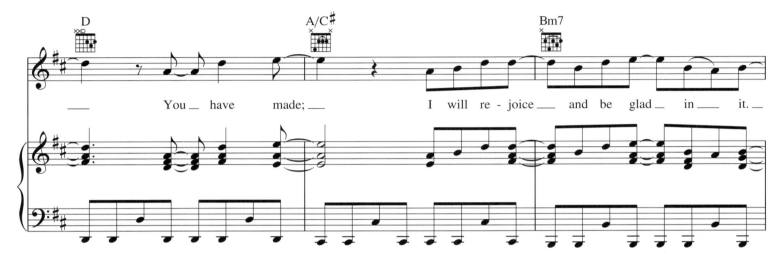

__ You __ have made; __ I will re - joice __ and be glad __ in __ it.

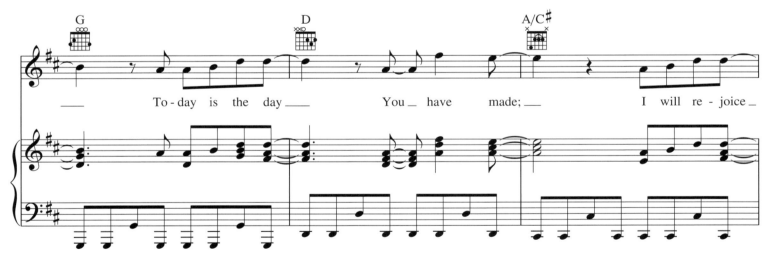

__ To - day is the day __ You __ have made; __ I will re - joice __

__ and be glad __ in __ it. __ And I _____ won't wor - ry __ 'bout __

____ to - mor - row, I'm trust - ing in what _ You say. ___ To - day is the day. __

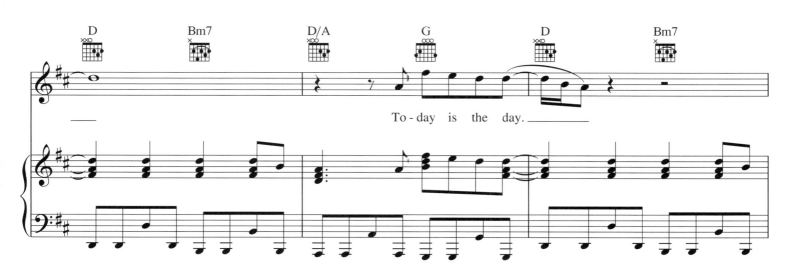

___ To - day is the day. _____

_I'm put - ting my fears ___

Guitar solo ad lib.

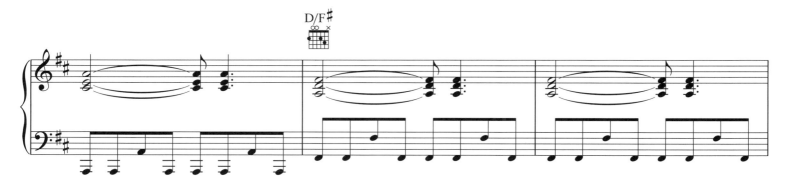

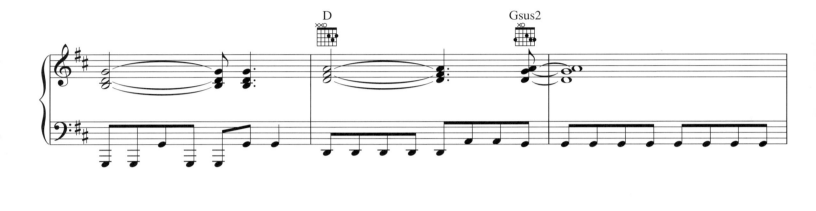

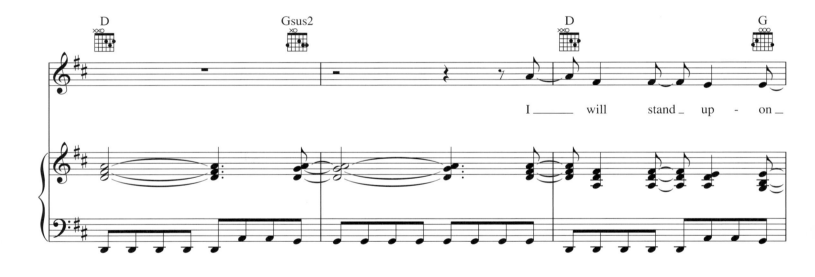

I _____ will stand_ up - on _

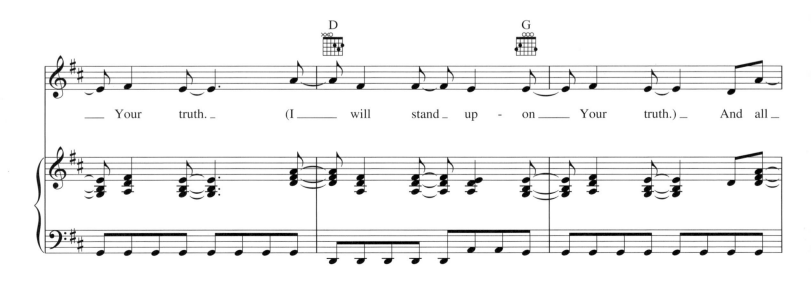

_ Your truth. _ (I _____ will stand_ up - on _____ Your truth.) _ And all _

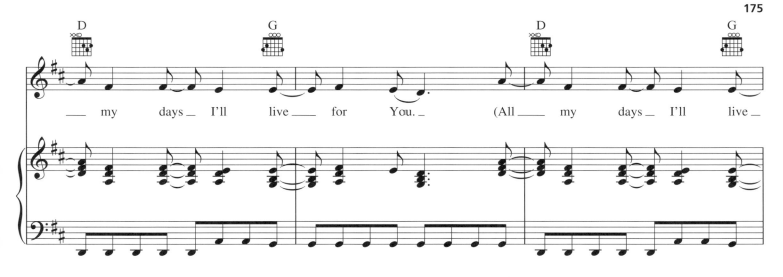

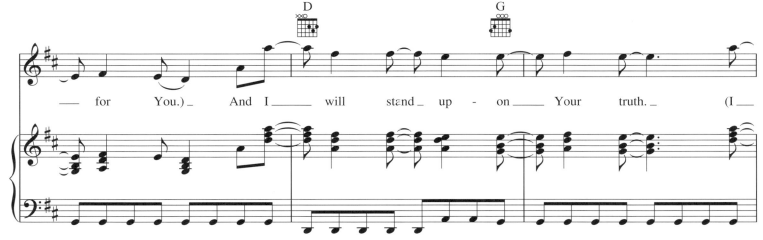

176

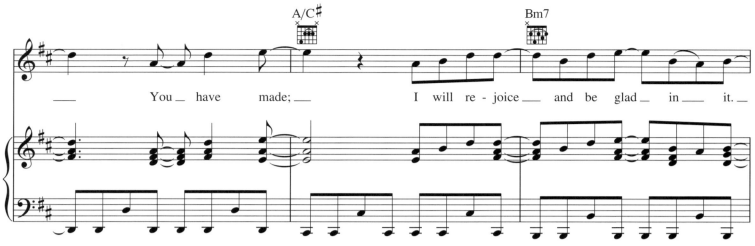

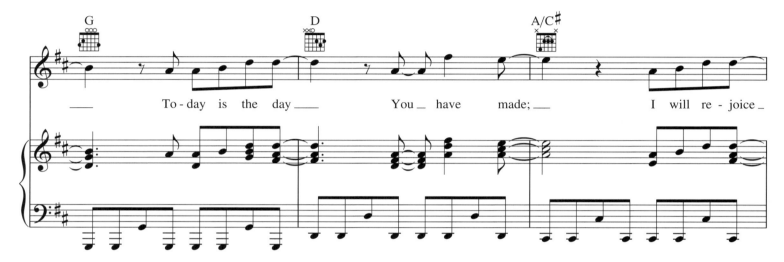

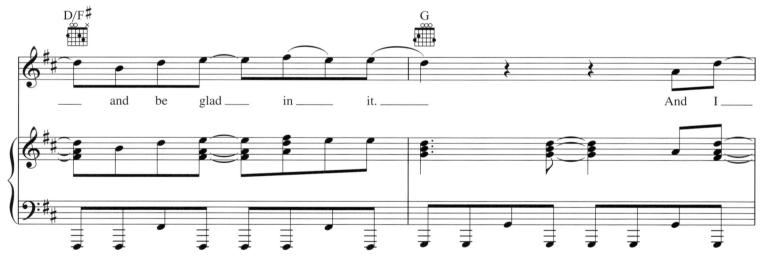

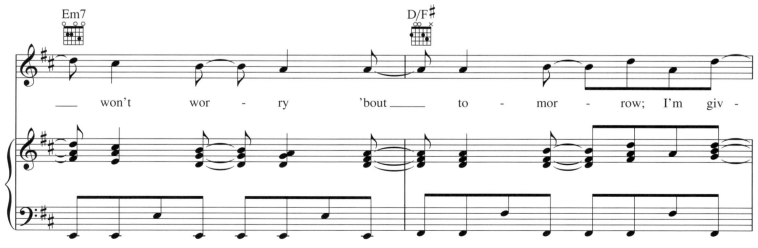

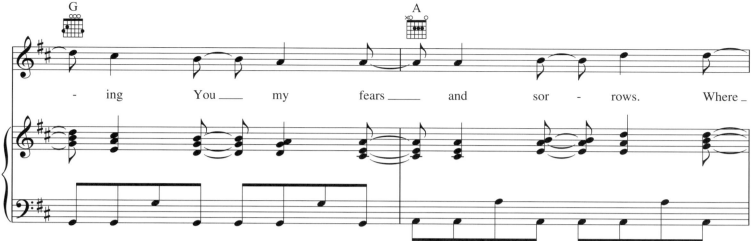

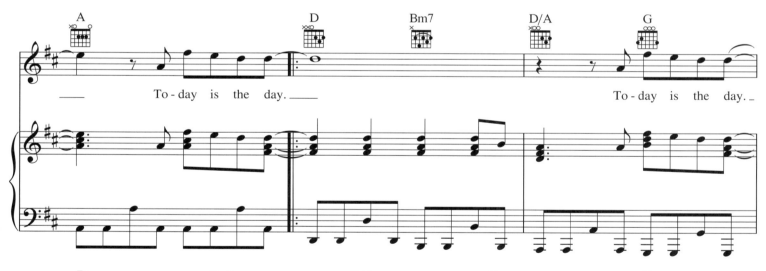

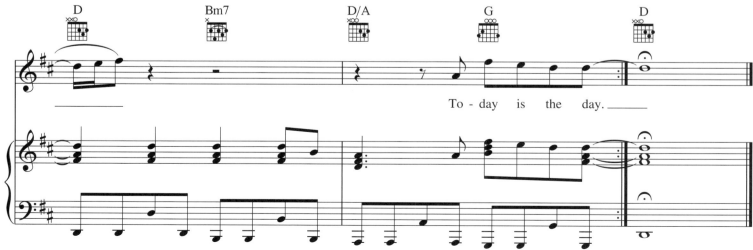

TRADING MY SORROWS

Words and Music by
DARRELL EVANS

Medium bright Rock

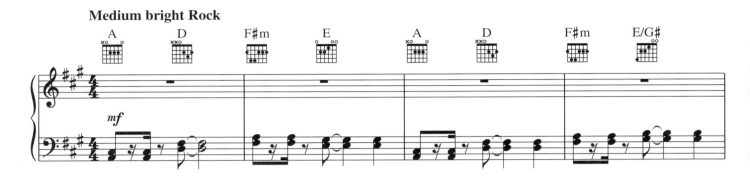

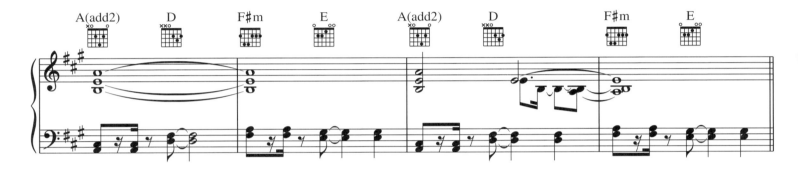

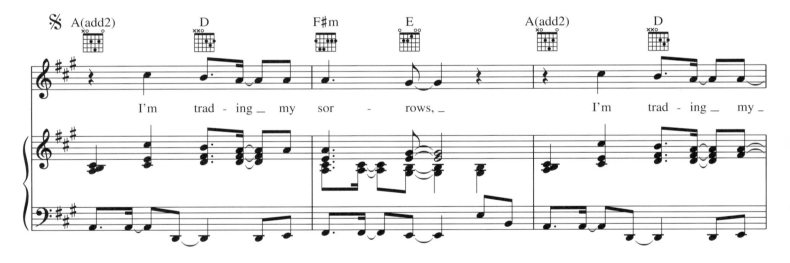

I'm trad-ing _ my sor - rows, _ I'm trad-ing _ my _

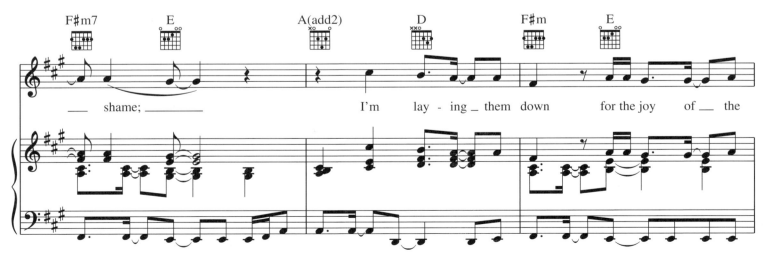

_ shame; _____ I'm lay - ing _ them down for the joy of _ the

yes, Lord, yes, Lord, yes, yes, Lord, _ yes, Lord, yes, Lord,

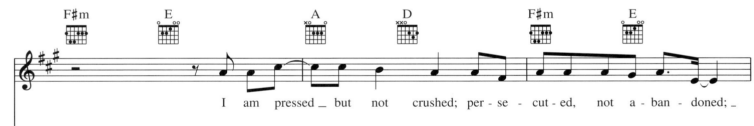

yes, yes, Lord, A - men. _____

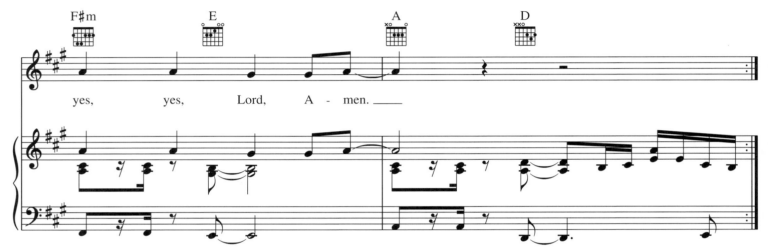

I am pressed _ but not crushed; per - se - cut - ed, not a - ban - doned; _

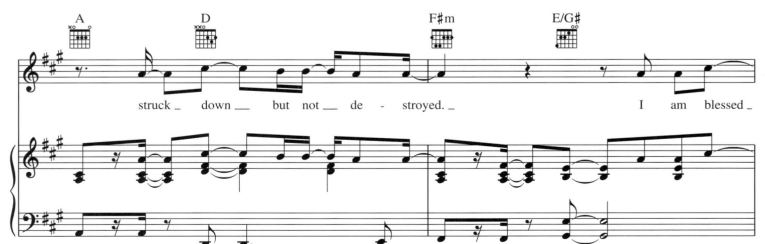

struck _ down _ but not _ de - stroyed. _ I am blessed _

182

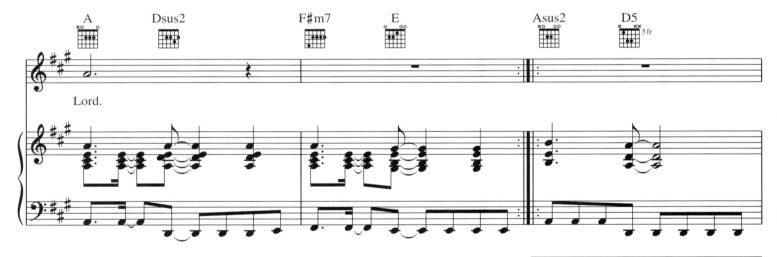

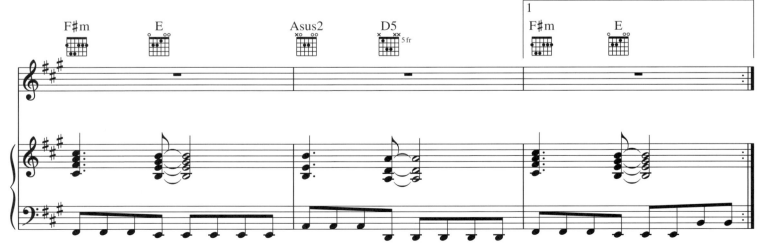

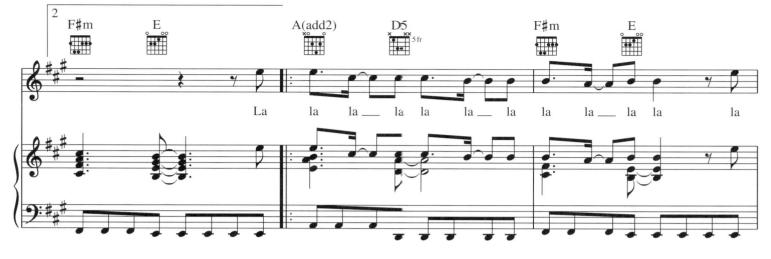

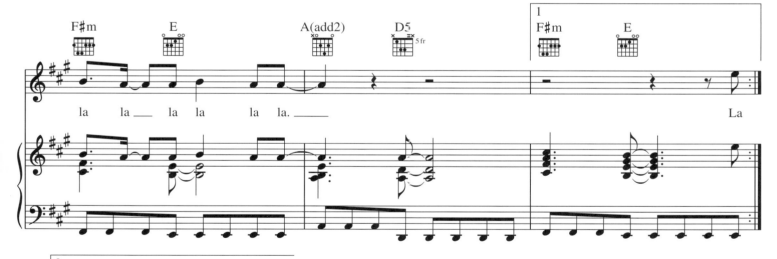

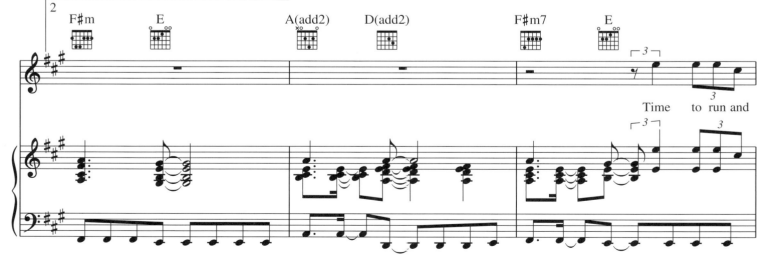

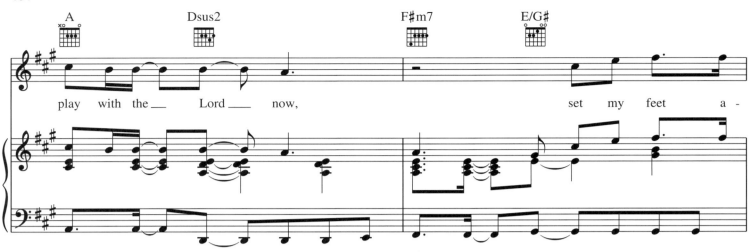

play with the __ Lord __ now, set my feet a-

danc - in', __ put a new song __ in my heart.

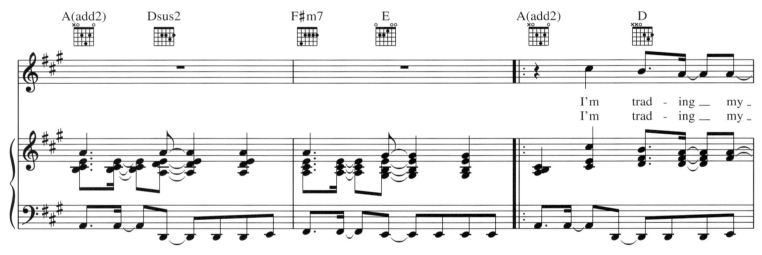

I'm trad - ing __ my __
I'm trad - ing __ my __

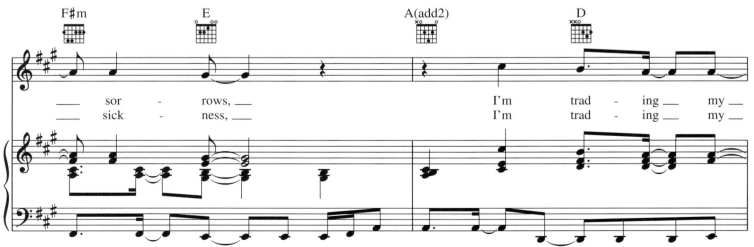

__ sor - rows, __
__ sick - ness, __

I'm trad - ing __ my __
I'm trad - ing __ my __

YOU ARE GOOD

Words and Music by
ISRAEL HOUGHTON

With energy

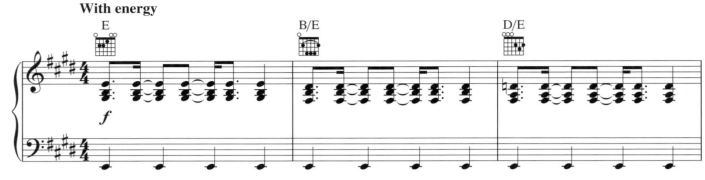

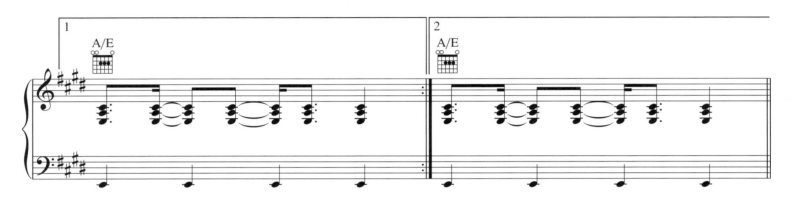

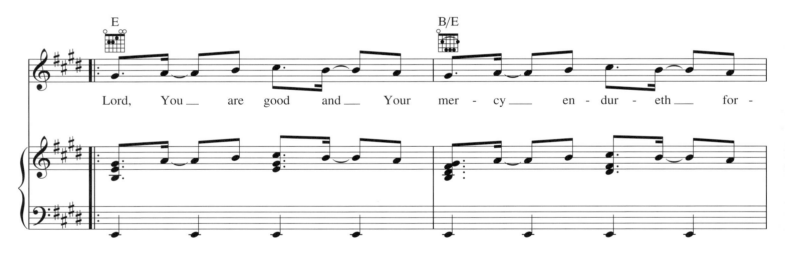

Lord, You __ are good and __ Your mer-cy __ en-dur-eth __ for-

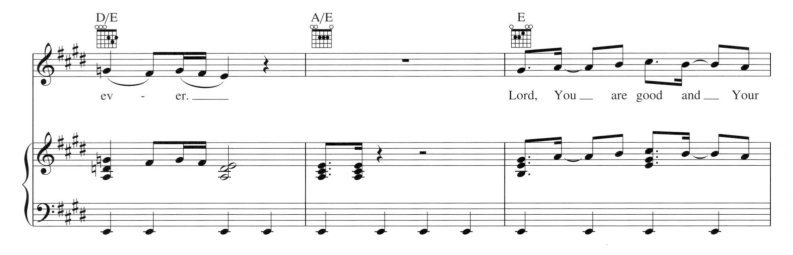

ev - er. _____ Lord, You __ are good and __ Your

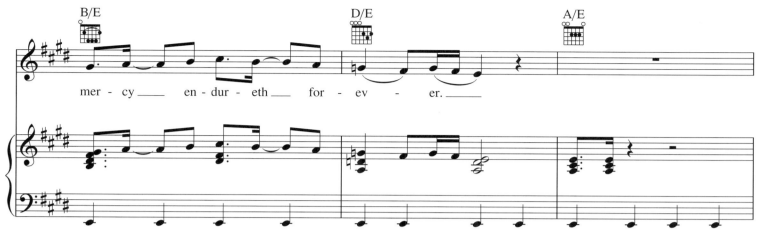

mer - cy ___ en - dur - eth ___ for - ev - er. ___

Peo - ple ___ from ev - er - y na - tion ___ and tongue,

from gen - er - a - tion ___ to gen - er - a - tion. We

wor - ship You, ___ hal - le - lu - jah, hal -

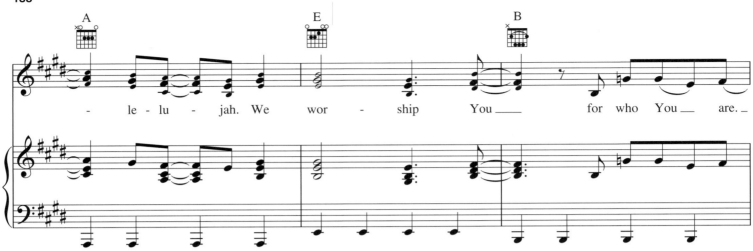

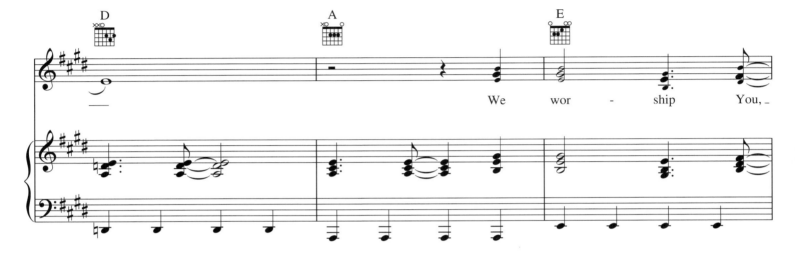

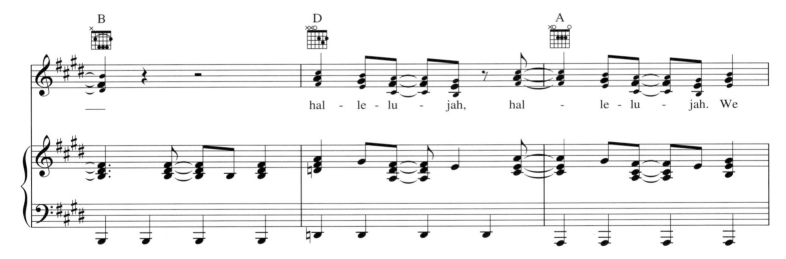

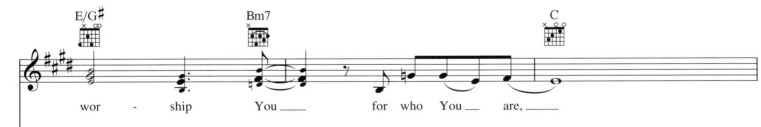

and You are ___ good. ___

So good, so good, so

good.

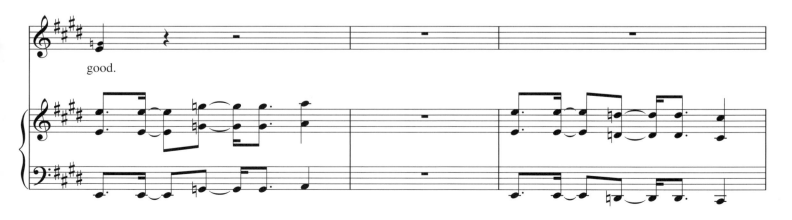

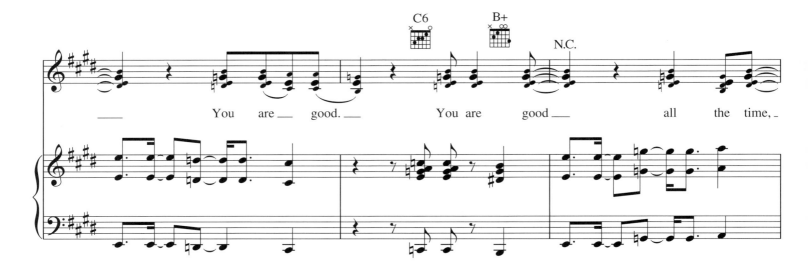

Lord, You __ are good and __ Your mer - cy __ en - dur - eth __ for -

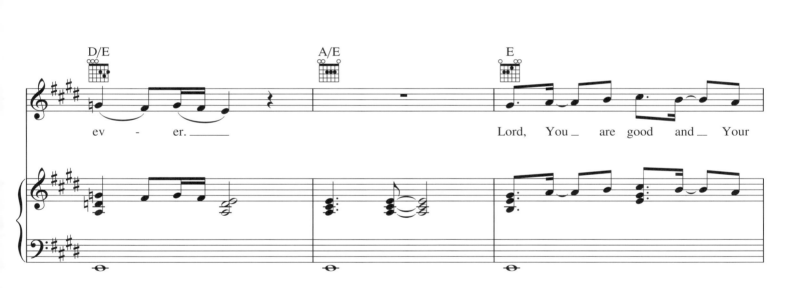

ev - er. __ Lord, You __ are good and __ Your

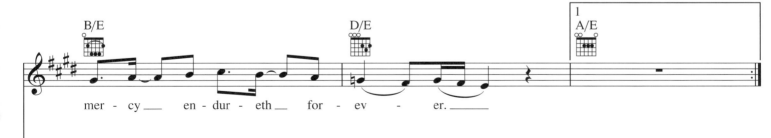

mer - cy __ en - dur - eth __ for - ev - er. __

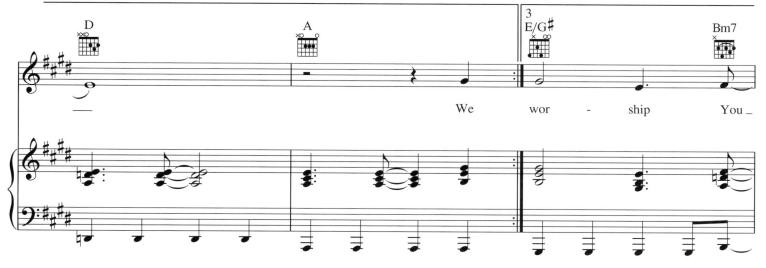

We wor - ship You _

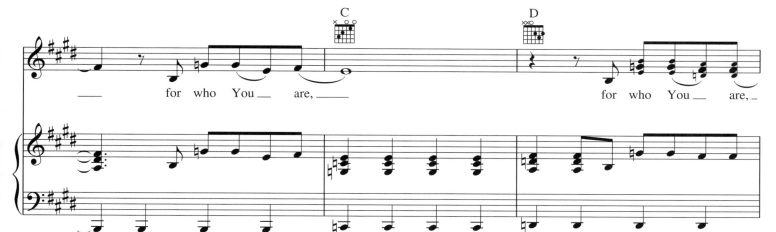

_ for who You _ are, _____ for who You _ are, _

_ for who You _ are, _____

and You are _____ good! _____

8vb

YOUR GRACE IS ENOUGH

Words and Music by
MATT MAHER

Joyfully

Great is ___ Your faith-
Great is ___ Your love ___

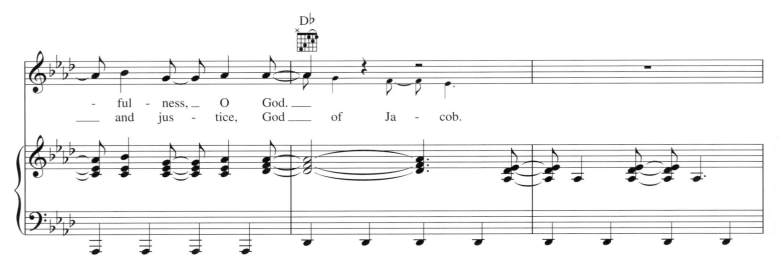

-ful - ness, ___ O God. ___
___ and jus - tice, God ___ of Ja - cob.

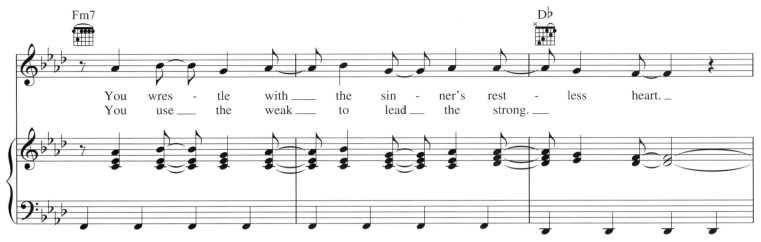

You wres - tle with ____ the sin - ner's rest - less heart. ____
You use ____ the weak ____ to lead ____ the strong. ____

You lead ____ us by ____ still wa - ters in -
You lead ____ us in ____ the song ____ of Your ____

____ to mer - cy,   and noth - ing can ____
____ sal - va - tion,   and all ____ Your peo -

____ keep us ____ a - part. ____
- ple sing ____ a - long. ____   So re - mem - ber ____ Your

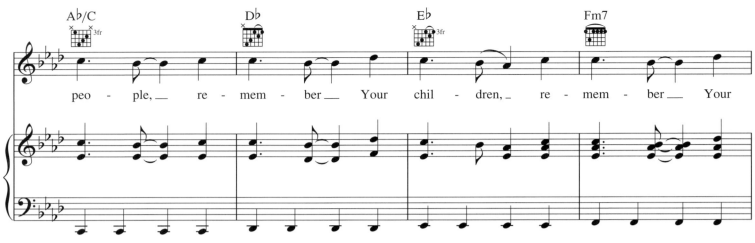

peo - ple, __ re - mem - ber __ Your chil - dren, __ re - mem - ber __ Your

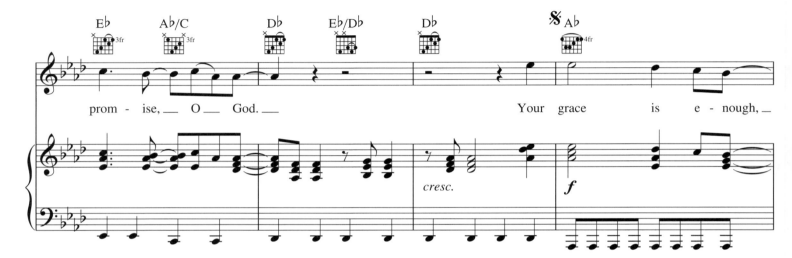

prom - ise, __ O __ God. __ Your grace is e - nough, __

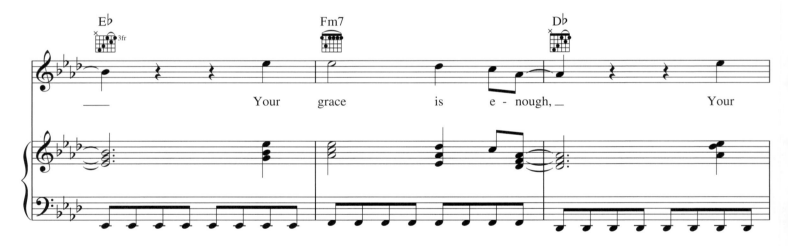

__ Your grace is e - nough, __ Your

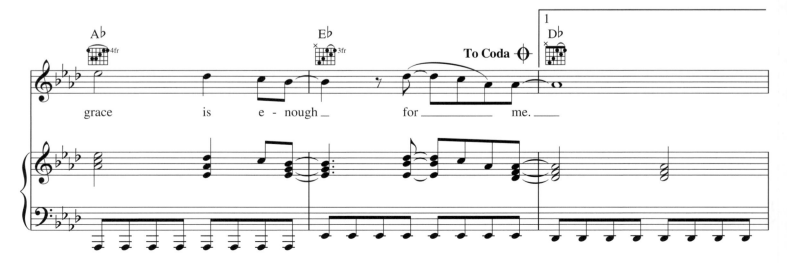

grace is e - nough __ for __ me. __

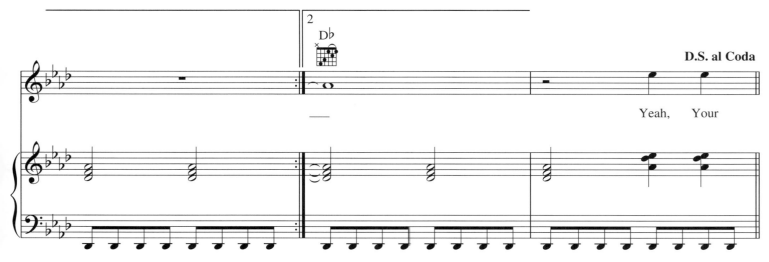

D.S. al Coda

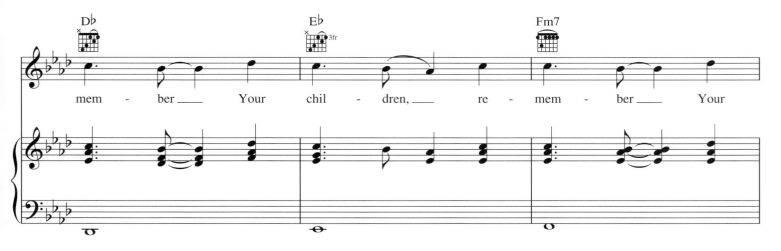

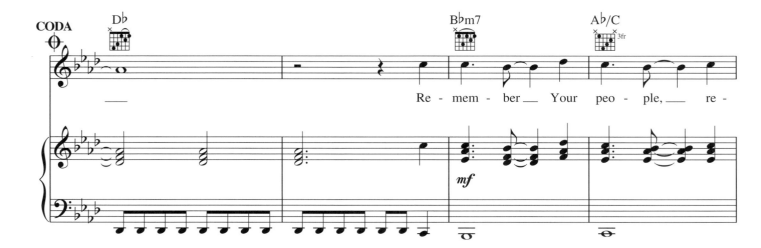

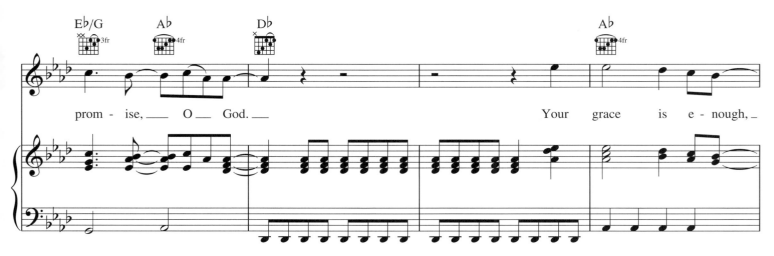

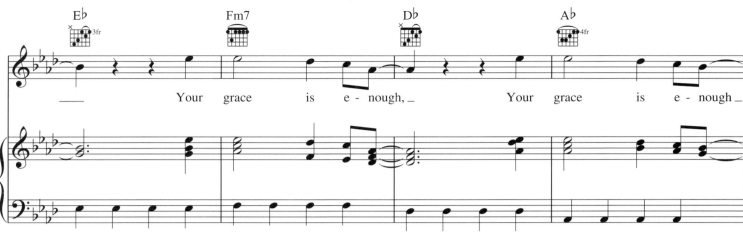

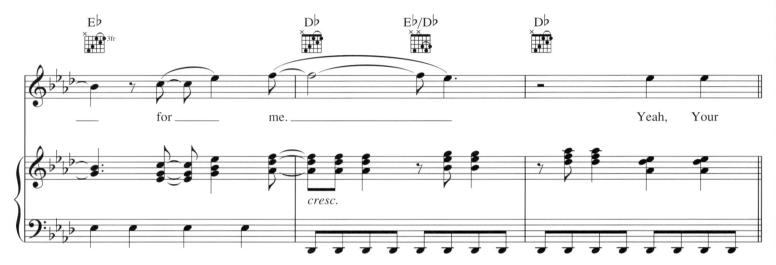

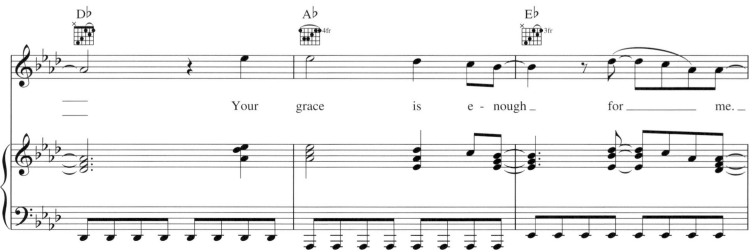

God, ___ I see ___ Your

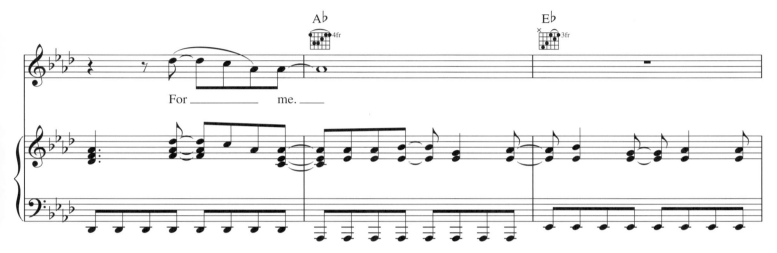

For ___ me. ___

It's e - nough ___ for me. ___

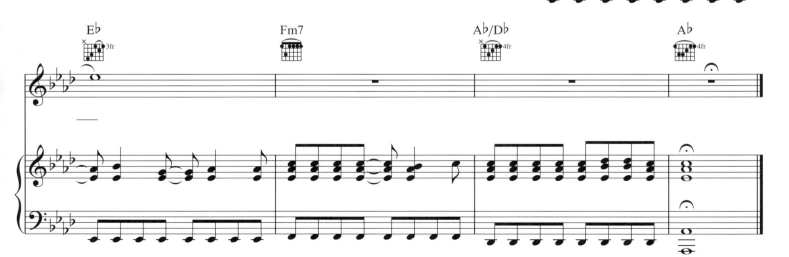

THE BEST PRAISE & WORSHIP SONGBOOKS

PAUL BALOCHE – OUR GOD SAVES

Matching folio to the live album recorded at his church in Lindale, Texas. 13 songs, including: God Most High • Great Redeemer • Hallelujah to My King • Our God Saves • Praise • Rock of Ages You Will Stand • The Way • Your Love Came Down • and more.

_____00306940 P/V/G......................................$16.95

LET THE PRAISES RING – THE BEST OF LINCOLN BREWSTER

Christian guitarist/singer/songwriter Lincoln Brewster was born in Fairbanks, AK but migrated to L.A., Oklahoma, then Nashville for his music making. This folio features Brewster's best, including the hit singles "All to You," "Everlasting God," and 14 more.

_____00306856 P/V/G......................................$17.95

DUETS FOR WORSHIP

Intermediate Level • 1 Piano, 4 Hands

8 favorites for worship, including: Above All • I Give You My Heart • Open the Eyes of My Heart • Shout to the Lord • and more.

_____08745730 Piano Duet $10.95

THE BEST OF HILLSONG

25 of the most popular songs from Hillsong artists and writers, including: Blessed • Eagle's Wings • God Is Great • The Potter's Hand • Shout to the Lord • Worthy Is the Lamb • You Are Near • and more.

_____08739789 P/V/G......................................$16.95

THE BEST OF INTEGRITY MUSIC

25 of the best praise & worship songs from Integrity: Ancient of Days • Celebrate Jesus • Firm Foundation • Give Thanks • Mighty Is Our God • Open the Eyes of My Heart • Trading My Sorrows • You Are Good • and more.

_____08739790 P/V/G......................................$16.95

COME INTO HIS PRESENCE

Features 12 beautiful piano solo arrangements of worship favorites: Above All • Blessed Be the Lord God Almighty • Breathe • Come Into His Presence • Draw Me Close • Give Thanks • God Will Make a Way • Jesus, Name Above All Names/Blessed Be the Name of the Lord • Lord Have Mercy • More Precious Than Silver • Open the Eyes of My Heart • Shout to the Lord.

_____08739299 Piano Solo $12.95

GIVE THANKS – THE BEST OF HOSANNA! MUSIC

This superb best-of collection features 25 worship favorites published by Hosanna! Music: Ancient of Days • Celebrate Jesus • I Worship You, Almighty God • More Precious Than Silver • My Redeemer Lives • Shout to the Lord • and more.

08739729 P/V/G....................................$14.95
08739745 Easy Piano.............................$12.95

THE BEST OF ISRAEL HOUGHTON

13 songs from the Grammy®- and multiple Dove Award-winning worship leader including his work with New Breed and Lakewood Church. Songs include: Again I Say Rejoice • Friend of God • I Lift up My Hands • Magnificent and Holy • Sweeter • Turn It Around • more.

_____00306925 P/V/G......................................$16.95

iWORSHIP 24:7 SONGBOOK

This album-matching folio features favorite worship songs by top artists, including: Again I Say Rejoice • Amazed • Hosanna (Praise Is Rising) • Love the Lord • Revelation Song • Your Name • and more.

_____00311466 P/V/G......................................$17.95

LET THE CHURCH RISE

25 Powerful Worship Anthems

This collection features: All the Earth Will Sing Your Praises • Days of Elijah • Hear Us from Heaven • Lord Most High • Shout to the Lord • Your Name • and more.

_____00311435 P/V/G......................................$14.95

DAYS OF ELIJAH – THE BEST OF ROBIN MARK

Robin Mark's worship music blends traditional Irish instrumentation with the passion of modern worship. This compilation features 14 songs: Ancient Words • Days of Elijah • Lord Have Mercy • Revival • Shout to the North • and more.

_____00306944 P/V/G......................................$16.95

THE SONGS OF MERCYME – I CAN ONLY IMAGINE

10 of the most recognizable songs from this popular Contemporary Christian group, including the smash hit "I Can Only Imagine," plus: Cannot Say Enough • Here with Me • Homesick • How Great Is Your Love • The Love of God • Spoken For • Unaware • Where You Lead Me • Word of God Speak.

_____08739803 Piano Solo.............................$12.95

MERCYME – 20 FAVORITES

A jam-packed collection of 20 of their best. Includes: Crazy • Go • Here with Me • I Can Only Imagine • In the Blink of an Eye • Never Alone • On My Way to You • Spoken For • Undone • Word of God Speak • Your Glory Goes On • and more.

_____08739862 P/V/G......................................$17.95

THE BEST OF DON MOEN – GOD WILL MAKE A WAY

19 of the greatest hits from this Dove Award-winning singer/songwriter. Includes: Celebrate Jesus • God Will Make a Way • Here We Are • I Will Sing • Let Your Glory Fall • Shout to the Lord • We Give You Glory • You Make Me Lie down in Green Pastures • and more.

_____08739297 P/V/G......................................$16.95

PHILLIPS, CRAIG & DEAN – TOP OF MY LUNGS

Our matching folio to the 2006 release by this popular CCM trio of full-time pastors includes the hit single "Your Name," the title song, and eight more: Amazed • Because of That Blood • I Will Boast • One Way • That's My Lord • more.

_____08745913 P/V/G......................................$16.95

Prices, contents, & availability subject to change without notice.

0208